How to Get A Sales Job

John P. Davis

©2020

Legal Disclaimer

ISBN 978-17-360-996-05

Connect with John P. Davis on LinkedIn or:

www.howtogetasalesjob.com

getintosales@gmail.com

How to Get a Sales Job, LLC

Dedication

This book is dedicated to my family.

They taught me how to sell.

"We must change our tactics or lose the game!"
– Abraham Lincoln

Table of Contents

Chapter 1: My Introduction to Sales

When I was twelve years old, my dad brought me to our local grocery store to apply for a job. The only opening for someone my age was bagging groceries. I didn't want to do it, but my dad told me that hard work would be good for me.

A few weeks later, I received my first paycheck and rushed out to the parking lot to open it. I don't remember the exact amount, but it was in the ballpark of seventy dollars. It was unreal. I was twelve years old with seventy bucks. I was rich.

I rode my bike over to the convenience store and bought a fresh pack of baseball cards and a Snickers. I wanted to buy a Pedro Martinez rookie card, but it was too expensive. I sat on a bench outside the store that afternoon, eating my Snickers and thinking about how cool it was to finally have my own money.

Then suddenly, it hit me. I wanted more. More money would give me more options. I could have bought that Pedro rookie card or maybe even gone to the mall to get a new bike. I started to think about how I could make more money at my current job. It had to happen.

My initial idea was to work more hours. I wrote my name down next to every open shift. I was excited until my manager told me that twelve-year-old employees could not work more than twenty hours per week. It was store policy.

My dad suggested that I ask about a promotion. If I were promoted to a position with a better hourly wage, I would earn more regardless of the twenty-hour limit. My manager broke the news to me again. In order to be promoted, workers had to be at least fourteen. I felt sick. I couldn't wait two more years.

My final idea was that if I worked harder than other baggers, the company would notice and pay me more based on my performance. It seemed logical. I began to bag groceries as fast and as efficiently as possible. I was one of the best baggers in Massachusetts. Sometimes, my manager even named me employee of the month, but a pay increase was never part of the picture.

My desire to earn more money never went away. I just suppressed that feeling and accepted what I was given. It was ingrained in me at a young age that companies had strict rules when it came to compensation, and I fell in line.

Career Steps

After college, I began working as a Financial Analyst, earning $38,000. I rented an apartment in South Boston and bought a used car. I started going out to dinner more often and hitting up Patriots games with my brother. The money was plenty for me because it was all I knew.

About a month into the role, something amazing happened. I discovered *overtime*.

I had accidentally worked forty-two hours one week and noticed that my check was higher than usual. After that, I worked forty-four hours, then forty-five. Eventually, I moved up to forty-seven hours and my checks increased.

But then my boss noticed. He told me overtime was monitored and I could not work more than forty-five hours per week. This conversation was strangely like the one I had as a bagger.

I had the same smart idea to seek out a promotion. I quickly found out that most promotions came after an employee earned a graduate degree. I just had to complete a nightly MBA program, consisting of six hours of class time per week for the next three years. I saw a path to more money, so I signed up.

Since my MBA would take time, I thought back to my idea that if I worked harder than my peers, management would pay me more based on my performance. Again, it seemed logical. Maybe they didn't reward performance at a grocery store, but they would at a bank, right?

Hard Work and Compensation

I worked directly with a woman on my team who was twenty years older than me. We shared the same job title and split

3

department tasks evenly each day. When finished, we reviewed each other's work and submitted it to management.

I worked diligently to ensure that I had no mistakes. At the same time, I noticed a lot of mistakes in her work. Eventually, she stopped reviewing my work altogether and my manager gave me more responsibility.

His appreciation of my performance was even more apparent after our annual review. He rated me five out of five and my colleague received a two. This confirmed that the company formally recognized my performance as superior to hers.

A few months later, our VP mentioned that my colleague was making double what I made. I wanted to throw up. The next day, I set a meeting with HR to ask how this could be possible. She had less responsibility and wasn't pursuing a degree. I was confused.

I was told that salaries were directly correlated to tenure. Because my colleague had seniority, she earned twice my salary. How could I increase my tenure without just getting older?

I was devastated. The bank was just like the grocery store. I waited to see if management would adjust the policy, but nothing ever happened. I was left hoping it would all work out somehow. Waiting around was a big mistake.

An Epiphany: Commission

Three years later, I completed my MBA and was now making around $50,000. One night over dinner, a coworker asked about my financial goals. I told her that my only goal was to make $100,000 by the time I turned thirty. She laughed out loud.

It seemed impossible. I started to feel pathetic. I could not keep waiting for something to happen. Then I had an epiphany.

I didn't need to make more money. I just needed to find a job that paid me more money based on my performance.

Did this type of job exist? I searched Google for "Which jobs pay you more money based on how hard you work?" I finally found the word I had been looking for my entire life…COMMISSION.

A commission is a form of payment from employers to employees based solely on an individual's performance.

This is what I needed! I needed to find a job that would pay me a commission. I found an article saying that commission was typically paid to employees with the job title, "Sales Representative."

Somehow, I needed to become a Sales Representative. Nothing else mattered to me.

It turns out that it's difficult to find a sales job overnight. It took me many failed attempts and awkward interviews before successfully becoming a Sales Representative. My failures were humbling. I learned a lot during my transition into sales, and I can honestly say that it was the best career decision I ever made.

A few years into my sales career, I thought back to my goal of trying to make $100,000 before turning thirty. I am fortunate enough to say that I surpassed my goal because I was now paid a commission. My performance at work finally mattered, and it directly affected my earning potential. It turns out that my dad was right all along. **Hard work does pay off… if you are in sales.**

While I continued to do well in sales, I could not help but be passionate about my transition. It helped me out so much financially and professionally. I wanted to share what I had done with others.

It did not start as anything formal. I began by coaching close friends on how to make a successful transition. I helped them with things like their resume and interviews, and what happened next was amazing.

First, I received a lot of praise from the people I helped as well as from their families, spouses, and even some of their parents. This alone was very rewarding. Secondly, I uncovered several best practices that helped make getting a sales job easier. Although each person had various levels of experience, I noticed certain elements that just clicked. These were aspects that were unique to the sales job application process and since they seemed to be repeatable, I formed a process to facilitate my coaching.

Once the word got out that I had developed a process, I found myself working outside my network. I was coaching random people I had just met. No matter who they were, I was able to guide them through my process and help them get a sales job.

I began receiving a high volume of requests for assistance. I was constantly explaining my process over the phone, so I decided to write it down instead. That is how I came up with this book. This is my tried and tested process of how to get a sales job.

Regardless of what point you are at in your career, you can use my process to navigate any sales job application process from start to finish. It directly reflects an actual sales process, and because of this, you can use it repeatedly. I refer to it as my sales job application process.

Learning it may feel new and uncomfortable at times, but just like my dad said, the hard work will be good for you.

John P. Davis

Chapter 2: A Sales Process

A sales process can be defined as a systematic approach involving a series of steps that enable sales reps to generate and close more deals.

Often, the series can be rearranged to cater to different industries, regions, markets, products, or any number of variables. Certain steps may vary from one sales rep to another depending on their preference or style. However, everyone in sales will agree that a sales process always involves four core components, which include **prospecting, providing sales material, meeting with prospects, and closing a deal.**

Because a sales process is based primarily on these core components, sales reps from all over the world can move between different companies and different industries and still succeed at selling all kinds of products. If you understand the sales process for selling software, you'll be able to learn the sales process for selling cars and vice versa. You will just have to be taught each respective process and work through it accordingly.

The best sales reps in the world are very good at following a sales process. You can drop them into any organization, provide them with the process, and they'll be ready to start selling.

Mastering every detail of a sales process will come in time with repetition. But if you focus on learning and executing the core components of a sales process, you can be successful in closing deals in any type of sales job.

A Repeatable Process

I have designed my sales job application process in a way that imitates the core components of an actual sales process. This makes it repeatable and unaffected by things like industry, company, or location. By designing it this way, candidates from all backgrounds can apply it to their search for a sales job with tremendous success. Just as sales reps can sell a wide variety of products by learning to follow a designated process, candidates will be able to secure a wide variety of job offers by following my designated process.

My sales job application process is broken down into five sections. In each section, you will be learning a series of steps that I will outline for you in great detail. They are directly correlated to the core components of a sales process. It is important to follow and apply each step from start to finish as my process builds exponentially upon itself.

By successfully completing my process, you will find yourself exhibiting behaviors and actions throughout your search that demonstrate you can follow an actual sales process. If you are deemed capable of following an actual sales process, sales managers from all over the globe will be more inclined to offer you a job. This is a fact.

Chapter 3: My Sales Job Application Process

You might be wondering why the ability to follow a sales process is so important to a sales manager during the sales job application process. Not many people have made this connection to date, so let's look at it together in more detail.

A sales job application process is much different than any other type of job application process. It is different because the decision to select a candidate is never based solely on credentials or qualifications. A sales job application process is exclusively based on a *real-time* evaluation from the sales manager as to whether a candidate can follow an actual sales process.

A typical job application process is structured in a way where you fill out an application, attach your resume, click submit, and then wait for a response from the hiring manager. If they like what they see, you will hear back. They will invite you in for an interview where you will discuss your achievements, education, and other relevant qualifications. If these credentials are above average compared with other candidates, you will most likely receive a job offer.

This type of job application process might be applicable if you were applying to be, say, an accountant, web developer, or financial analyst. I am not trying to speak poorly of other professions. I am simply outlining the typical framework that you would encounter when applying to most open jobs on the market. The only job where this type of job application process does not apply is a sales job.

Sales Hiring Is A Unique Process

In sales, the application process is not as straightforward. If you were to submit an application, attach your resume, click submit, and then wait for a response from a sales manager, the odds are high that you'll never hear back from anyone.

Why is this the case in sales and not in other professions?

It is primarily due to the high number of discrepancies surrounding a candidate's credentials as they relate to sales ability. Let's look at two quick examples where subjectivity on credentials come into play.

There is no way in the world for a sales manager to determine if a graduate from Princeton with a 3.4 GPA in History will be any better at cold calling prospects than a graduate from UMASS with a 3.8 GPA in Economics.

There is also no way to determine whether a sales rep who achieved 148% of quota at Yahoo will better a better addition to the organization than a sales rep who achieved 139% of quota at Microsoft.

Credentials Are Subjective

Things like education, past job experience, job titles, achievements, and yes… even annual performance are subjective when evaluating candidates during a sales job application process. It is impossible to determine whose qualifications are better just by looking at a piece of paper.

People may argue that Princeton and Microsoft are more mainstream and more established household names; therefore, those candidates must be better suited for the sales job. This is indeed true in other professions but not in sales.

For example, an accounting degree from Princeton usually holds more weight than an accounting degree from UMASS. This is because of considerations like curriculum, rigorous coursework, and the overall quality of the faculty. Or say, if you were a financial analyst at JP Morgan with an MBA from Stanford, you would most likely be looked at as more qualified than a financial analyst at a local credit union without a graduate degree. This type of information is not highly regarded in sales because credentials are subjective and not a strong indicator of sales ability.

I have seen it first-hand. An MIT graduate was hired into an entry-level sales role at my prior company. A few weeks into the role, his manager came to me very flustered because his new rep was afraid of making cold calls. In fact, the rep refused to make any calls at all! I asked why he was hired if this were the case. His manager told me, "I just figured he'd be good because he went to MIT."

Subjectivity regarding a candidate's education is apparent, but it doesn't stop there. Subjectivity is also evident when considering past performance. For instance, I interviewed a sales rep who had listed 249% of the annual quota achievement on his resume. When I brought him in for an interview, he was so excited to tell me that his 249% of quota was made up of one big deal. He was so proud of this deal, so I decided to see how it unfolded.

After five minutes, I was able to figure out that this deal was initiated by one of his coworkers two years prior. The entire sales cycle was run by his Senior Vice President. He even admitted that he did not have much involvement in the cycle and was just "a passenger along for a heck of a ride." So, on paper, this candidate was 249%, but if you remove this one deal (where he admitted *he did not contribute*), he would have achieved 0%. This is one clear example as to why past performance is subjective in sales.

The point is not that these things do not matter at all. It's rather that information on a piece of paper can be very misleading while evaluating sales candidates.

When it comes to other credentials, job titles can also be misleading. How can a manager determine if an "Account

Executive II" at SalesForce will turn out to be better than a "Named Account Manager IV" at Oracle? There is no way to distinguish between job titles because every company has its own nomenclature and ranking system. The titles may be based on things like sales experience, company hierarchies, or performance, but sometimes they are just irrelevant naming conventions altogether. It is dangerous for a sales manager to base his or her opinion on titles.

Having seen many more similar examples, I can confidently state that education, experience, achievements, job titles (or any other type of credential that you think may separate you from the pack) will not help you in a sales job application process. You may think they will, but that's a common misconception among candidates.

With credentials being a non-factor, or at the very least subjective, candidates find themselves trying to navigate the sales job application process in many different ways. They try several approaches yet are always left wasting time, wondering how to differentiate themselves. There is only one way to separate yourself from other candidates, and it is through *proactive demonstration of action.*

A Proactive Candidate

A sales manager may not come out and actually say it, but he or she is always looking for a candidate who can come into the organization, learn the specific sales process, and follow it repeatedly to generate more revenue for the company. End of Story.

This is the only thing that a sales manager is looking for in a candidate during the sales job application process. Even if the sales manager talks about having other standards, the ability to consistently follow a sales process is the only thing that actually matters to them.

I never met a sales manager that cared about your GPA. I never met a sales manager that was interested in your job title. I never met a sales manager who cared if your internship was at a Fortune 500 company or at your Uncle's company.

I should clarify - I have never met a <u>good</u> sales manager who cared about any of those things. Occasionally, you will come across a poor sales manager who hires solely based on subjective items (like the manager who hired an MIT grad because he went to MIT). If you find this to be the case, trust me, you would not want to work for this type of manager. You will come across these types of sales managers, so it is important to be aware of them.

Poor sales managers care more about what kind of watch you wear rather than how many prospects you met with. Their organizations are typically more focused on trying to impress senior management in ways unrelated to revenue. They look to hire reps from brand name companies with 10+ years' experience because it "looks good." Poor sales managers are more interested in their outward appearance versus how to better enable their reps to carry out the company's sales process.

It is important for you to avoid these types of managers. If you find yourself speaking with someone who is focused on how good you look on paper, you're in the wrong spot. This is key because if you are hired by one, you will find yourself coming back to my sales job application process sooner, rather than later, to pursue another new job.

You only want to work for a good sales manager. It is often better than working for what people consider to be "a good company." Sales managers matter. The ones who enable you to carry out your sales process more efficiently are the ones who will help you make more money. So, if a good manager cares more about the process than credentials, how do you demonstrate that you can follow a sales process?

Well, you could just come right out and tell them you are good at it...

This happens a lot, and it's a very common approach I see with candidates. I have interviewed many candidates who will explain to me in detail just how great they are when it comes to following a sales process. When I hear this, I will put them to the test and request a follow-up email on three specific items that we talked about during the interview. Once we are done with the interview and talking about how great they are, the candidate will close me, shake my hand, smile, and leave. And then I never hear from them again.

When a candidate tells me that they are very process-oriented but never cares to follow up on items that I specifically ask about, it is a huge red flag (as it should be). If you do not have the sense of urgency to follow up with me, there is a high probability that you will not have the sense of urgency to follow up with our prospects.

I am very direct with candidates who don't follow up with me after interviews. They usually tell me that they act differently in front of prospects than they do in interviews. With prospects, they always stick to the process, but with me, they forgot to follow up because they were busy with something else.

Therein lies the fundamental problem with candidates during the sales job application process. **Actions speak much louder than words.**

If you are going to be applying for a sales job, you must carry yourself like a sales rep throughout the entire sales job application process so that you properly demonstrate through action (not words) that you are capable of following a sales process from start to finish.

I realize that it may sound cliché to identify the lack of follow up as a reason for not hiring a candidate. However, during the sales job application process, I have witnessed candidates miss on all kinds of different parts of a sales process. I have had candidates not close me, show up late to an interview, forget their resume, and I have even had candidates be rude to our receptionist. I have observed candidates doing a million things that directly demonstrated to me that they were incapable of following a sales process from start to finish.

From the moment you decide to begin searching for a sales job, you must be able to demonstrate your ability to follow a sales process. **It can only be done through action.** Your credentials, your performance, and what you bring up in conversation are all going to be subjective. Your actions will be the highest weighted part of any sales job application process, but no one will ever tell you this. It is the best-kept secret in sales. Your actions are the only measurable indication of how you will act and interact with customers, prospects, and sales management if given the job. I will walk through how to put your actions to work for you, and you will begin to see the results firsthand.

I have worked with candidates from all over the world who have had many different levels of sales experience. I have coached everyone from University Students to Senior Sales Executives. A candidate's experience was rarely an issue. The only issue was how these candidates acted and carried themselves. My process lets you demonstrate through action that you are capable of following a sales process despite your background or lack thereof.

I learned this through many years of observation. If that does not seem scientific enough for you, you are probably in the wrong business. Selling is not scientific; it is process-oriented. If you can learn a sales process, all you must do is repeat it until you sign a deal. If you can learn my sales job application process, all you must do is repeat it until you sign a sales job offer.

I will leave you with this. One of my clients was a hostess with no sales experience. She was able to get a high-tech sales job in London by following my process. In her final interview, the head of Sales told her, "I'm not sure how you got this far along in our application process, but we really like how you've carried yourself. I shouldn't do this because of your experience, but we'd like to make you an offer."

The Five Sections

When each section of my process is combined into one natural series of steps, you'll be able to demonstrate to a sales manager through action that you are capable of prospecting, providing sales material, meeting with prospects, and closing a deal.

Resume

We'll start by building out your **resume** so that it is suited for sales. By completing this section, you will <u>demonstrate</u> that you can provide clear, direct, and relevant sales material to prospects.

Branding

We will then refresh your social media, phone skills, and email etiquette to ensure that your online and personal brands are on par with sales standards. By completing this section, you will demonstrate that you understand the importance of having a professional brand while interacting with everyone you encounter in the sales world.

Targeted Networking

We will then set up a list of target companies and learn how to interact with their employees to set up a phone interview. This is what I refer to as Targeted Networking. By completing this section, you will demonstrate that you know how to handle all communication and follow up with prospects in a professional manner.

Phone Interview

We will next examine all aspects of a Phone Interview, which is a scheduled conversation with the sales manager. By completing this section, you will demonstrate that you know how to meet with prospects and run a sales call effectively from start to finish.

In-Person Interview

The In-Person Interview should be run in the same manner as a sales meeting with a prospect. Most reps are amazing when they meet with prospects, but struggle in front of someone who could be their new manager.

I will teach you how to treat each type of meeting with the same sense of urgency. By completing this section, you will demonstrate that you can run a sales meeting effectively and close a prospect in person.

I am excited to walk you through each section in detail. Once you learn my process, I think that you will be excited to go out and use it in the real world.

Chapter 4: Resume

Have you ever opened an email from someone you didn't know and saw five paragraphs of text? This is the fastest way for me to hit delete. How about those "one-liners" that say, "15 minutes can save you 15% or more on your car insurance"? While this might be a solid tactic for a commercial, it is not going to warrant many callbacks. It is too short and too specific.

Then, there are those emails that just don't make any sense at all. Sometimes you see these hit your inbox and wonder if it was even intended for you in the first place. Delete.

A sales rep depends on sales material to repeatedly penetrate companies and generate demand for their product. Successful sales material should present a clean and direct message that causes the prospect to call or email the rep back. It should not be too long, too short, and definitely not too complicated.

Most companies have a team of people that work on building out high-quality sales material for their sales reps. If companies left this task entirely up to the reps, a lot of them would overcomplicate or miscommunicate the material. The only goal behind sending out sales material is to generate a positive response from prospects that result in a request for the next steps.

Once you decide to start looking for a new sales job, people will ask, "Can you please send me your resume?" This is the equivalent of a prospect asking a rep, "Can you please send me more information?" It is just that in this case, your resume is now your sales material. This is what you need to depend on to repeatedly penetrate companies and generate demand for yourself as a sales candidate.

You do not have the luxury of having a team of people who can help you build out a high caliber resume, so it is in your best interest to spend some quality time with me revisiting the fundamentals to ensure that your resume is focused on getting a sales job. I will show you how to structure your resume in a direct and relevant way so that it generates a positive reaction when presented to anyone that you may encounter during the sales job application process.

There is no other point to a resume than to generate a request for a meeting. While a creative resume may demonstrate your personality, the resume we build will demonstrate your ability to provide prospects with direct and relevant sales material. A good sales manager will notice the difference between the two.

Your Name

The way that you present your name on your resume should be the easiest and most straightforward item, but it's often overlooked. When you overlook things, you miss out on opportunities to take advantage. Your name is the first opportunity on your resume to present yourself to other people, and more specifically, to the sales managers who will eventually be deciding whether to hire you.

Does the presentation of your name really matter? Yes, it does. On your resume, your name is your *first* "first-impression" to a reader. It is essentially what you are selling. Your name is your product. There are two goals you should focus on when it comes to presenting your name. You must present it with confidence, and you must present it in a way that does not distract the reader.

I typically see resumes come across my desk where a candidate's name is formatted in 9 pt. font on the top left side of the page. This format tells me that I am about to read the resume of an introverted candidate. It does not tell me that I am about to read the resume of a confident and bold sales rep. It also fails to demonstrate the candidate's burning desire for my attention and leaves me wondering just how eager they are to join my organization.

You can tell a lot from someone's font and size choices; just ask the FBI. They analyze these things all the time. All of this occurs to other sales managers and me within one second of glancing at the page.

By not formatting your name in a confident manner, it is a missed opportunity. If this were your sales brochure, you would be sure to showcase your product's name, confidently, front and center. Yet, for some reason, sales candidates instinctively shy away from calling too much attention to their name on a resume. Why? It is essentially the same concept. You are trying to sell a product, and you are trying to sell yourself.

Keep in mind that the other side of this coin can be just as telling. A massive, bold, and bubble-lettered name set to 42 pt. font tells me that you may be a narcissist or way over the top. This could turn off a reader. There are some areas in sales when being over the top might make sense, but your resume is not one of them.

Your name should appear a little larger than a 12-pt. font. It should be in the center of the page and can even be bold if you like (but not overwhelming). Your name is unique, and it is part of your identity. Stand proudly and make it a proper header on your resume.

My name appears as John P. Davis in 22-pt font. I include my middle initial because "John Davis" is very common. I added the "P" to differentiate myself.

You do not have to include your middle initial. You can if you think it will help you stand out in a crowd, but it is by no means a requirement. There are no real rules as to how you must format your name as long as it fits my rule of being confident and not distracting.

How can your name be distracting? If your legal name is long and most people refer to you by a shorter name, I recommend using the shorter name on your resume. I had a friend in college named "Oluwaseun," who went by "Seun." It helped keep conversations flowing naturally without having to explain the origin of his name each time he was introduced. He did not have anything against his given name. Making it shorter was just a way of keeping things moving. It may not be a huge distraction, but length should be considered when presenting your name on a sales resume. If people call you Gwen, you do not have to put Gwendolyn on your resume.

For those of you who are concerned with accuracy, let me tell you that it is not an official requirement to list your legal name on your resume. I know that your legal name is technically correct, but your resume is not an official job application. The application comes later.

Please… no nicknames, no gimmicks, and *definitely* no lies. Anything like that will just get you in trouble. All you must do is format your name in a confident manner that presents you as a strong sales professional without distraction.

Contact Information

In terms of providing contact information, most candidates tend to include a wide range of details at the top of the page. It is usually crowded and gives off the impression that the candidate is disorganized or has difficulty summarizing information.

The more phone numbers, zip codes, apartment units, and hyperlinks you try to squeeze in, the more attention it demands from the reader. If a reader is required to process a bunch of detailed information upfront just to understand where you live and how to contact you, you're putting the time spent on the rest of your resume in jeopardy. A reader's precious time should be spent reviewing your sales skills, but instead, you have called their attention elsewhere.

Sales reps are not as detail-oriented as you might think. They are more into the big picture and summaries.

The only three items that you should include as your contact information are an accurate email address, an accurate phone number, and your current location. That's it. Let's take a look at each item.

Email Address

It's important to use an email address that does not contain a ridiculous name. This should be common sense, but an email like julie@hotmailfuntime.com instantly tells the reader that you are unprofessional, lazy, and probably unaware of your surroundings. These qualities are undesirable in sales, and you will most likely not receive a callback.

Imagine if you reached out to the CFO at Bank of America trying to set up a meeting, and you included this email address. The CFO would think it was some sort of scam and never respond. If it affects you this much in a sales cycle, it will have the same impact during your sales job application process.

The best thing to do is to create a clean and professional email on gmail.com. Gmail is the industry standard, and it's free. By setting up a dedicated Gmail account solely for this process, you can use it repeatedly to correspond with your network, gatekeepers, and sales managers confidently. This should be the only email address you list on your resume. You would never provide a prospect with more than one email address. Why do that here?

You will be communicating via email frequently throughout my process, so it's important to have a dedicated email to keep your correspondence consistent, timely, and effective. If you miss a sales manager's email or fail to respond, you are crossing yourself off the list of potential candidates. This happens quite often when candidates rely on multiple inboxes.

By having a dedicated Gmail you also mitigate the risk of accidentally replying to a sales manager from julie@hotmailfuntime.com. This stuff happens. Please take your email address seriously and spend five minutes setting up a new Gmail account as part of my process.

Phone Number

Surprisingly, most candidates manage to mess this up. It seems impossible, but it happens all the time. If a candidate is struggling to provide their phone number properly, you can imagine how quickly a sales manager will stop reading.

If you are applying for a sales job within the same country where you currently live, then you do not need to include a country code. I have seen candidates list out something like

+033 1(166) 414-2810 when they are applying for a job in their hometown.

This is not insignificant because it can tip off an above-average sales manager that you don't have much common sense. This is the equivalent of texting your sister and telling her to go to https://www.google.com instead of just telling her to Google it. It instantly gives off a strange vibe, and most managers will start to look deeper into your resume for other signs of strange behavior.

If you are applying for an *international* sales job, it is acceptable to include the country code at the beginning of your phone number.

Sometimes candidates will list their phone numbers with extensions. If you do not have a direct cell phone number, please go out and get one. Do not list a phone number that has an extension, and never list the phone number to your desk at your current job.

There is no need to list a cell, home, and work number. This just makes this section busier and suggests you are not up to date with current methods of communication. Imagine if you gave a prospect three different phone numbers to call. What would they think?

The only goal of your phone number is to provide someone with an easy and accurate way to contact you by phone. That's it. Don't make it more complicated than it is.

Current Location

I do not have enough time or space in this book to explain how much irrelevant information I have seen regarding a candidate's current location. Honestly, almost anything that candidates include here will be overkill.

Sales managers don't need to know your home address. They don't need your P.O. Box number or your extended zip code. They *definitely* do not want to see your latitude and longitude (true story, I saw this before). I don't know if they thought it was funny or not, but I immediately thought, *"No, thank you,"* and moved on to the next resume. It made the candidate seem as though they might not be self-aware, and self-awareness is key for a successful sales rep.

Some of you may be questioning my decision to pass on a candidate based solely on their contact information. *"Perhaps this person was just being extremely detailed and should not be penalized."* However, sales managers are not looking for this type of candidate. This type of candidate would become the type of rep who lists the dollar amount on a contract down to the third decimal point because they think that rounding numbers is incorrect.

These minor but strange tendencies will eventually rub a prospect the wrong way and jeopardize a deal. Sales managers look for candidates who can provide summarized and direct messages to prospects in an effective manner. Extreme care for detail can be counterproductive in sales. If a sales manager can identify this type of rep by simply looking at a resume, it's better time management to move on to another candidate.

When it comes to your current location, I think it is best if we all just agree that your city and state are the only details that really matter. No one needs to know your actual home address. No one is ever going to read your resume and start to draft you a letter. They just want to know what part of the world you live in. Also, sales jobs often require travel over larger geographic regions. If travel is a big component, your exact address may not be as important as you think.

If you are worried that you may advance further in the process to a point where you will be asked to prove that you have a home address in a certain city, that's okay. It's easy enough to do this later with HR. For now, you are not that far along in the process where it matters, and your resume is only being used as a sales tool to send out to other people. If those people have questions, they will reach out and ask you. That's when you can discuss the details.

Social Media

Other trendy items are becoming more prevalent in the contact information section, mostly related to social media. Candidates now include things like the URL for their LinkedIn profile or their Instagram and Twitter handle. When it comes to my process, please do not include this type of information on your resume. It can only hurt you.

For starters, links and URLs take up too much space. If I want to find you on LinkedIn, I can go to LinkedIn.com and find you within a minute. If you include a link simply for the reader's convenience, it's not a good reason. Sales managers will be able to find you regardless of this information and you are just adding too much unnecessary text to the page. White space looks cleaner.

When it comes to adding your Instagram or Twitter handle, no good sales manager is ever going to think, "Wow, let me look at her Instagram and see how many likes she has!" And no good sales manager is ever going to pull up your Twitter and think, "Wow, he has some really good retweets about sales. I love the content." These reactions are highly unlikely, and other more realistic reactions could be detrimental.

People may argue that social media is relevant today in sales and that candidates should be proud to showcase their content. However, when you are applying for a sales job, social media cannot demonstrate your ability to sell. It only leaves you exposed to criticism. Having a strong social media following does not demonstrate anything related to your ability to follow a sales process.

It could show that you have a good network, but that is not a great reason to hire a rep. Healthy activity on Twitter will never demonstrate to a sales manager that you can cold call or progress a sales cycle. Process demonstration should be your only intention. If a piece of information cannot accomplish this, and you choose to include it on your resume, you are opening the door for unnecessary judgment.

Social media can be a great complement to your sales process later on, but the best practice is to exclude it in your contact information because there is no way to predict a sales manager's reaction to it. Think back to all those other platforms that were once considered "the be-all, end-all," like Facebook. Today, not many people consider Facebook relevant except for your parents who post political memes. If you included Facebook on your resume today, a lot of sales managers would question your intention.

What's to say that those same sales managers wouldn't question your Instagram or Twitter handle the same way? There is simply no way of knowing how a sales manager will react to your choice to include social media. Therefore, by omitting it from your resume, you are mitigating risk and improving your chances of moving forward in the hiring process.

When it comes to your basic contact information, please just include your cell phone, a professional email address, and your current location. This will put you in the best (and most risk-free) position of moving forward in the sales job application process.

Summary

A summary on your resume should be two sentences that summarize your current situation and state your purpose. It is meant to be short and impactful and summarize your situation with intent. That's it. There is no secret sauce here.

You probably scan through lots of mind-numbing information every single day. Maybe you scroll through your texts, newsfeed, or Instagram. At some point, your eyes will relax and wait for something to pique your interest.

The same thing happens to gatekeepers when scanning through resumes. It's a mundane task. The sheer volume of information blends everything together. **This blending makes a Summary on your resume 100% necessary.** Gatekeepers scroll through resumes all day looking for outliers and for others that boldly state, "I am a good sales candidate." A Summary is the best way to literally GRAB a reader's attention.

If you were a sales rep, you would be sure to include a summary of your product, so prospects wouldn't have to dig through details to understand what you're offering. As a candidate, you should do the same.

Most candidates who include a summary tend to ruin it with too much fluff. Fluff can best be described as those common and overused catchphrases like "Self-Starter," "Motivated," or "Driven." This is about as captivating as writing "Funny," "Cool," or "Hot" on your Tinder profile. These phrases are generic and show little effort. It bores me when I read ten resumes, and nine of the candidates are "motivated and enthusiastic self-starters."

When I see fluff in a candidate's summary, I take a couple of things from it. First, I know that the candidate was smart enough to understand that a summary is impactful and necessary to capture a reader's attention. While this may be a good start, it also tells me that they do not have enough confidence to separate themselves from other candidates. This distinction is a quality that all sales managers are looking for in a sales rep. In sales, the skill to be bold and noticeable carries its weight in gold.

A great sales rep will never generalize his or her sales messaging to prospects, especially when it comes to the actual headline. These reps will make it direct, relevant, and personal. If the headline on sales material is just fluff, the prospects will be left wondering what the intended message is and what kind of action is required on their part.

It may sound obvious, but it should also be adaptable. You should never apply for a Pharmaceutical Sales Rep position with a summary that states, "Looking to join a high-tech Fortune 500 company." You will not get a callback. Worse, you will always be left wondering what you did wrong. One day, you might realize that your summary was written for tech sales by mistake, but by that time, it is too late to do anything. Candidates waste weeks and even months waiting to hear back from companies when if they had just taken time to prepare their material accordingly instead, they'd be in the driver's seat.

Additionally, your summary should be short and sweet. If your current circumstance seems particularly extenuating, and you feel that you have a lot to explain, please take a deep breath and refrain from doing it in your summary. I encourage you to do any type of extra explaining in-person once you are invited in for a meeting.

If you use your summary to try to explain why you took six months off to train for Muay-Thai boxing in Thailand, you are increasing the odds that your resume will be left in the dust. Salespeople are looking for reps who are clear cut in their messaging. If you start off by explaining a ton of details, you are getting off on the wrong foot. Please try to **only use two sentences to describe who you are and what you want from a reader.**

I suggest running a draft by one of your close friends. When you are asking for help, I recommend phrasing it like this, "I am trying to describe who I am and what I want to do in only two sentences. Can you help me paraphrase this?". If you frame up the ask this way, you will receive more direct and better feedback.

I have helped Sales Executives who manage a $200 million book of business re-write the summary on their resume. I only point this out because it can be a tall task for even the most seasoned sales professionals. The ability to summarize and captivate a prospect or reader's attention is one of the most important components for becoming a top sales rep. It takes practice, and it is an art to be captivating but not overwhelming.

Candidates often ask me, "If I'm just supposed to be clear and direct, why don't I just write this?"

SUMMARY: I want this job because it's a high paying sales job at a reputable company. I am the best sales rep at my company, and I would be a great addition to your organization.

If you are following my process exactly as I have laid it out, this might be what you come up with. I told you to be bold and direct in two sentences. So, this summary fits the mold. But it does it in a negative way. Even if it is true, your summary should never be *this* bold and direct. You want to be sure that you state your intent in a respectful manner with just a hint of your own color.

In terms of color, if there is something specific that differentiates you, be sure to include it. I have clients that start their summary with, "Dual citizen looking to…". I have other clients who will add in phrases like "Willing to relocate…" or even "Former US Marine Captain…". This is the one spot on your resume where you can captivate a gatekeeper with very few words. These example phrases are short, but they are compelling pieces of information.

If you do not have something like this to include, please do not try to make something out of anything. I would advise against things like, "Former high school track star…" In the example where my client used, "Former US Marine Captain…", it was five months after his service. If you are going back to high school athletics to set yourself apart, and it was over ten years ago, you are reaching. You just need to add an effective statement as to who you are and what you want to do. There is no need to reach back to the "glory days" to find something. Be current. Be relative. Be direct.

Take your time with your summary and remember to run it by a close friend. This is your statement of purpose. Make sure it's impactful. If you don't include a summary, you are never going to capture someone's attention.

If you are new to sales, this might feel a little strange. It might feel like you are leaving too much out or that you are too direct. But trust me, when you are looking for a sales job, this is considered a perfect start. You are being straight to the point and leaving the door gently open for more conversation.

If you are already in a sales role, you might be thinking, "What am I doing reading this guy's book? This is so basic. I learned this in middle school."

I'd argue that my ideas are not basic at all.

What I am teaching you here is to be aware of the little things that even the best candidates take too casually. These little things are the first impressions a gatekeeper will see when looking at your sales tool. It's important to get them right. A good impression is everything, especially in sales.

Imagine you are a rep who finished at 117% of quota, and you decide to pursue a new sales job at Apple. You're feeling confident about your achievement and think that it will carry you throughout the process. However, your name, contact information, and summary appear as follows.

John Davis   Work: 1 (492) 555-2101

85 Albany Cul-de-Sac, Unit #231-22a   Mobile #: 1 (402) 555-8962

South Hampton Beach, Long Island, NY   Home: (510) 555- 1508

04102-02949

https://www.linkedin.com/in/john-p-davis-548a7b22/

Twitter: @sales-john50

Summary: Motivated self-starter who is driven and carries himself with an overly competitive nature. Former Division 1 Athlete (Men's Tennis D1AA) who focuses on overachieving on quota consistently.

What do you think the VP of Sales at Apple will think of your 117% achievement when this is the first thing they see on your resume? The truth is that they might not ever see that you finished at 117% that year because they'll stop reading after seeing this.

If you're accustomed to this approach, my example might not seem that bad to you. However, a sales manager who reads dozens of resumes a week will almost certainly pass on this resume. This resume is not a great sales tool. I know plenty of sales managers that would skip over it.

Experience

The Experience section is meant to provide a reader with your professional experience to date. We are going to take it a step further and use this section to demonstrate that you have the relevant skills of a high-performing sales rep. To accomplish this, we must shape your experience in a way that shows you can follow a sales process and generate revenue. This section is where candidates run the highest risk of ruining their chances of moving forward in the sales job application process.

I am still amazed at what I find in a candidate's Experience section. From brand new candidates to even the most seasoned reps, the content is never consistent and rarely focuses on the sales process or sales activity.

I assume the inconsistencies stem from there being too many sales resume experts available today. The problem with listening to one expert over another is that each person's advice is usually very specific. By using specific advice, you will only be targeting a specific percentage of sales managers. Your goal should be to target your resume towards the highest percentage of sales managers. That would be the definition of a best practice.

Rather than debate what makes up the highest percentage of sales managers on the market, it's better if we focus on what I consider to be the good sales managers. A good sales manager is one that enables reps to repeatedly run a sales process and generate revenue for the organization. Therefore, a good sales manager will be looking for resumes focused on the sales process and sales activity. By applying this concept to each job within your Experience section, you will be targeting good sales managers. In my opinion, these are the only ones that matter.

It's important to remember that you never want to cater to nor work for a poor sales manager. Life is too short to work for a poor sales manager. I could go on at length, but I won't. Just understand that if a sales manager is interested in things outside your ability to perform sales activities, they are not worth your time.

Before I get into details on how to structure this section appropriately, I will explain a bit more about the philosophy of what to avoid.

What Not To Do

When I see a candidate's resume hit my inbox, it usually takes me about thirty seconds to lose interest. I spend twenty seconds skimming the name, contact information, and summary, and then I immediately jump to their Experience and ask myself, "What type of sales activities do they have experience with?"

This flow is the equivalent of a sales manager opening the door to their office and saying, "Hi, it's nice to meet you. I just read your summary, and it sounds great. Can you please let me know what type of sales-related activities you have experience with?" Picture yourself in that situation. This hypothetical situation is the exact thought process taking place in a sales manager's mind when they get past your summary. At this point, they only want to learn about your past sales experience and related skills.

What happens 99% of the time is that the rest of the resume is full of all sorts of insignificant facts. Resumes are filled with irrelevant job duties, confusing job titles, and extremely specific dates of employment. I am not kidding when I tell you that I have seen everything from an Algebra calculation outlining a detailed quota assignment all the way down to an explanation behind the science of metadata management. Sometimes I don't even know what I'm reading!

Think back to the real-life example of a manager opening their office door to greet you. Would you use that opportunity to jump into some type of discussion around metadata? Of course not! So why do it on your resume? Even the most seasoned sales reps struggle. I once had a recruiter send me a resume from someone who was applying for a Key Account Sales Rep position. This rep would be covering one of the best accounts at our company, and the average salary was north of $300k.

Not more than five lines down the page, this candidate had "Equestrian Jockey" listed under experience. He included a bullet point that read, "Jockeyed for my Equestrian Team in High School." The applicant had been out of high school for almost thirty years at this point.

Maybe he thought that Equestrian Jockey would be an eye-catcher for a sales manager. But to other good sales managers, and to me, it was an eyesore. It appeared as though he hadn't updated his resume in almost thirty years! There was no need for this. I instantly dug deeper and found more details that proved he had put no thought into his resume.

To be clear, I do not toss out a resume as soon as I come across something that deviates from the norm. This is an exercise in understanding what *not* to do. If you are trying to land an interview for a Key Account Sales role with a highly competitive salary, it is best practice to leave off a three-decade-old data point like "Equestrian Jockey." To the critics who claim these types of fun facts should be included, I will explain later how and where to add interesting information like this, but the Experience section is not the place

The Experience section is also not a place for you to list all those funky one-off jobs you've had, either. Many candidates (especially recent grads) will list every little thing they've ever done here. When I ask why, they say things like, "What if HR eventually checks and sees that I was a cashier at that arcade four years ago?"

That is attempting to plan for outliers. You are assuming the thoroughness of the company's HR department. You are also assuming that even if this comes up, it might somehow matter to the sales manager involved in the hiring process. When it comes to structuring your resume for sales, these things simply do not matter.

I worked in a chocolate factory when I was nineteen. I do not put this on my resume. If HR ever dug into my employment history and asked why I didn't include working at a chocolate factory on my resume, I would be able to explain it.

There is a huge difference between leaving something off your resume and leaving something off your job application. Your resume is a sales tool and meant to be abbreviated to showcase your relevant sales experience. Your application is an official document for Human Resources' records.

Don't ever lie on an application. Please take this seriously. Your application and your resume are two different things. Omitting an old job from your resume is not lying. It is a sales tool used to grab the readers' attention. But omitting your previous job from an application is lying. Be practical here and think through what to include and not include on your resume.

There may be situations where you were at a job for two weeks. I advise you to only include this if it was somewhat recent. For me, recent means within the past four years. Prior to that time frame, it is up to you to use your own discretion.

Common Sense

Please don't ever do something like put on your application that you were never arrested because you read this book. This is not the point I am trying to make. I don't feel like I need to get into the weeds of what to include and what not to include on an application versus a resume. I am just saying that you should be aware that the Experience section is where you want to explain relevant and recent sales activities that you think matter to a sales manager. Your application is where you must be more official with job history. If you get in the habit of lying or embellishing to make yourself look better, you will crash and burn faster than you think. Please use common sense.

If you leave off that you were an alternate Ballerina for the Nutcracker in 2001, that is fine. But if you omit that you were terminated from a sales job for stealing, you are going to get in trouble. The Experience section of your resume is not meant to be used as a job application. It's important to understand the difference.

Building Out Sales Experience

What should your Experience section actually be used for?

To start, you need to address all the following questions for every job you've had before. Don't worry about structuring it yet. Just focus on answering thoroughly.

- Where did you work?

- What are the sales-related activities that applied to this job?

- Did you stand out?

- Why did you leave?

If it helps to answer in complete sentences, you can start by doing so and then shortening your answers to bullet points later.

To the veterans who are rolling your eyes, I still encourage you to answer these questions to start. You will find this helpful but also a bit confusing because you are used to doing things differently. You are used to doing things the old way, by putting in your attainments and where you finished against your quota. In fact, you might even ignore this part of my process altogether because you think that you already know what you are doing. This exercise will open your eyes to a new way of building out your career story. It will provide you with a much stronger sales tool and will undoubtedly lead you to more job offers.

Let's first start with the question about where you worked. All your answers will include information like the **Company Names, Job Titles, Locations, and Dates of Employment.** It is very straightforward. A typical answer might be, "I worked at IBM as a Junior Sales Account Executive in New York City from May 2010 to November 2013."

This is how you would answer in a full sentence, and because all your answers will contain the same elements, you can structure each of as follows.

IBM - New York City, US	May 2010 - Nov. 2013
Junior Sales Account Executive	

Some candidates will want to top Lady Gaga here and go crazy with their formatting, but I disagree. A sales manager wants you to be clean-cut and direct. Anything else is considered a distraction, so please refrain.

Write the company name in bold, 14- or 16-point font to show that it is important and to make it stand out. It is one of the <u>most</u> important pieces of information for you to display. Format the location and work dates in 10- or 11-point font and be sure to abbreviate things where appropriate. Dates and city names can sometimes make the section too busy for readers. Words like November and North Dakota can easily be shortened to Nov. or N.D.

Underline your job title because there will typically be bullet points that fall directly beneath the line. Underlining is crisp, clean, and under control. Italics never work on a resume. Don't use them. It is out of place in sales. Remember that your resume is a sales tool, not a screenplay.

Job Titles

The idea of writing down your Job Title sounds easy. Go ahead. Think of your current Job Title and write it down somewhere.

I don't even know you, but I can tell that I probably don't like what you wrote down.

I am overly critical when it comes to Job Titles. They are a huge pet peeve, and the one thing I hate discussing with candidates. It pains me when I hear people tell me their Job Title. I cringe when I see their email signature or what they list on LinkedIn. Why? I have seen hundreds of job titles for people who claim to be in Sales, and each title is used to cover up this fact.

Most people do not want anyone (especially not prospects) to know that they are in sales. For some unknown reason in society (especially in business), "Sales Rep" has become a bad word. Look at what you wrote down as your Job Title. I guarantee you did not write Sales Rep. If you did, I'm proud of you and somewhat shocked. No one ever refers to themselves as a sales rep.

Years ago, I was at a company where I was a top Sales Rep in North America. Around this time, I was approached by another rep who was struggling to sign any deal. He said, "I think you should take 'Sales Rep' out of your email signature. He told me, "It looks too salesy. I put something else in mine, so I sound important like I'm not in sales." This was crazy to me.

I always tell people I am a sales rep. I am proud of it, and at some point, I'd like to have a business conversation about the exchange of goods and services for money. I like to talk about contracts. I'm not a consultant. I like dinners and coffees. I'm not technical. I make it very clear who I am and what I want from prospects.

Most salespeople do not want to admit this about themselves, and it bothers me. They want to appear more important, just like that guy. They want to hide the fact that they sell things or the fact that they are going to ask you to sign a contract someday (like it's such a bad thing). This guy did not tell anyone that he was in sales. I sold a lot. He did not sell much. He eventually quit. Maybe if he had told prospects that he would like them to buy something from him, they would have done so.

If this guy thought that by referring to myself as a "Sales Rep," people would think I'm trying to sell them something - then great! **You should do this on your resume.** Maybe a sales manager or two will see that you are trying to sell things! This is part of my process. Refer to yourself as a Sales Rep! Show that you are not afraid to tell people you are in sales. It's a good thing. A sales rep is one of the highest-paying jobs in the world. Do not hide the fact that you are in sales to anyone.

If you are a sales veteran, this is where you may blush a little and still prefer to shy away and refer to yourself as something else. If you are brand new to sales, this is a good lesson for you to learn. Regardless of your experience level, I encourage you to never again refer to yourself as one of the following Job titles:

- Senior Account Executive
- Sales Development Advocate
- Named Account Manager
- Passionate Conversation Haver

Okay, so I made that last job title up. I have never seen Passionate Conversation Haver. I hope I never come across it in the future, but I have seen all those other job titles and probably a few more that I have forgotten to list. They are cringeworthy, and they prevent people from knowing you're a sales rep. Stop using them.

Seriously. Especially with social media today, it seems like everyone is trying to be anything else but a Sales Rep. People want to be sales reps, but they don't want to tell people that they <u>are</u> a sales rep. You are here because you are trying to get a sales job, so why don't you try the following process and take my advice?

Tell your friends, tell your family, tell your network, tell gatekeepers, tell sales managers, and tell everyone that you want to be a sales rep. **There are too many wannabe account managers in this world and not enough wannabe sales reps.**

When someone asks you what you do, be proud to tell them that you are trying to get a sales job. Sales reps are extremely successful. It is okay to say this, and it is okay to publicly declare that you are a sales rep.

On your resume, I encourage you to use Job Titles down that show that you were some form of Sales Rep, or Inside Sales Rep, or Financial Services Sales Rep, or any other kind of Sales Rep at your prior company.

"But what if I'm not in sales?"

I understand how you feel, and believe me; I hear this often from candidates. Remember that there are two types of people reading this book. There are those who are brand new to sales and those who are already in sales in some capacity. If you are one of those who are brand new to sales, let's start by looking at how you should handle your current and previous job titles. We will get to how it applies to sales veterans later.

Brand New Sales Job Titles

If you are brand new to sales, you must remember that you must think and act like you are already in sales. The best way to think about this is with the age-old Garbage Man example. If you are currently a "Garbage Man," you will want to list your job title on your resume as a "Waste Services Representative." By doing this, you are actively associating your current job title with the sales industry.

If you sell hot dogs at Fenway Park, you should now consider yourself a "Concession Sales Representative" This is actually a job title that I've dealt with in real life. I worked with a candidate who sold hot dogs at Fenway Park every summer while in college. After he landed a high paying sales job, he said that his new job title on his resume was a great talking point during the process.

If all else fails and you are having trouble finding the right job title, my recommendation again is to run it by a friend. I used to make the mistake of putting all kinds of weird things in my job titles to make them seem more prestigious or more "senior." However, I have learned over the years that what you want to do is make it short and specifically related to being a sales rep. This packs the most punch on your resume and makes it stronger.

The point is not to lie or confuse the sales managers. Rather, the point is to use a bit of the English language to help assimilate your current position to a sales position. This assimilation will go a long way in grabbing the sales manager's eye. Too many beginners will shy away from writing "sales" in their job title. I understand that it may be intimidating to take this step, but remember, you are building a sales tool. It is important to use your space wisely.

Seasoned Sales Job Titles

For those sales veterans out there, I encourage you to think twice about your job titles in your Experience section. Your current and previous roles will already have specific job titles, and I bet you even signed an offer at your company that had those titles specifically called out. However, there is no need to list this exact title on your resume. Why shouldn't you list out the exact job title that you were given?

Maybe an "Account Executive" at Microsoft is a different level than an "Account Executive" at SAP. Maybe a "Business Development Rep" at Amazon is actually higher than an "Account Manager" at Fruit of the Loom. Because these types of job titles are specific as they relate to each company, there is no way of knowing which is better or worse. This could be a problem for you.

For instance, there may be times where a "Senior Account Manager" at your company is the highest-ranking sales role. But when you apply to a new company, their position titled "Senior Account Manager" is actually considered a much lower role than a "Principal Sales Executive." You might be highly qualified for their "Principal Sales Executive" role but are weeding yourself out by holding true to the naming convention at your own company. A busy sales manager might pass on your resume after quickly seeing your title. It's possible.

There are hundreds of examples of this type of situation where a gatekeeper or sales manager might think that your job title isn't the right fit for the open role because it is just not clear to them what it actually means.

I once worked at a company where I was technically referred to as a "Technology & Application Digital Sales Representative

III". I was just an Inside Sales Rep, but this was my company's specific job title.

I remember one interview where a sales manager asked me, "What is a Technology & Application Digital Sales Representative III?" I was so embarrassed. She took her time saying it, and it sounded so bad.

I stammered, "…um… that's what we call it… but I'm actually an Inside Sales Rep". She nodded. She now understood my role. We eventually found common ground because she was once an Inside Sales Rep. In the future, I wanted to avoid this unnecessary questioning and get straight to the point. It made me wonder how many other sales managers were confused by titles.

You do not want gatekeepers and sales managers to go on a wild goose chase, trying to understand what it is you do in your role. Everyone reading your resume will understand that there are different naming conventions, so it is important for you to generalize the titles so that they understand how it conforms with their company's titles. Stick to the most commonly used titles such as Business Development Rep, Inside Sales Rep, or just Sales Rep for anything else. If you want to put "Senior Sales Rep" or "Field Sales Rep" instead of just "Sales Rep" because you think it makes a difference, just know that it might make a difference, and the wrong type of difference is the one we're trying to avoid.

In the past, I have had recruiters send me resumes where a candidate had only listed "Sales Rep" as their job title. The recruiter told me they were sending it my way because they were unsure what level the candidate was at based on the title. But because they saw that the candidate was in sales, they wanted me to review the resume anyway. **This candidate's generalized job title alone had made the recruiter curious enough to move them along in the process.**

Sales-Related Activities

Now that your company name, location, dates of employment, and job titles are squared away, this brings us to the most highly debated bullet points on your resume: the points meant to explain your duties and responsibilities.

We have already answered some of the questions about where you worked above. Your answers to the remaining questions will eventually become these highly debated job duty bullet points.

What should you put for these bullet points? How do you convey power and authority, right? What are the best action verbs that are captured by SEO? How many bullet points should you have? Five, six, seven, or eight?

This is the most difficult part of a resume for sales reps.

The reason why this is so difficult is that, again, there is too much advice out there. There are so many "best practices" and "new buzz words" for the strongest bullet points needed to

catch the eyes of a sales manager. But I am here to tell you…
stick with me. I know what sales managers are looking for—and
it is nothing like what you have ever heard before. I literally sat
down to write a book about this stuff because it is so important
to me, and no one else explains it like this out there.

The material that I am going to have you list is probably
considered edgy because it is not typically what you will hear
from "the experts," but I can say with confidence that my clients
have a higher probability of receiving a callback or receiving an
invitation to interview when they follow my instructions.
Landing more callbacks and interview requests should be your
only goal.

I will start by recommending that you only include two to three
bullet points underneath each job title.

*"But what if I did way more than that, and I can't fit it all in two or
three bullet points?!"*

I don't care. Neither does the sales manager. Talk about those
extra points after you are invited in for an interview.

The two exceptions here are related to the number of jobs you
have had. If you have only had one job or are a recent graduate,
you will want to include five to six bullet points to fill an entire
page. If you have had over five jobs, you will want to keep it to
one bullet point for each job only as a way of keeping it to one
page.

For the record, I have had eight jobs and am still able to fit my entire resume on one page by using one to two bullet points for each job.

Now that we agree on the number of bullet points, what do you put for each bullet?

Your bullet points should only contain sales-related activities that you performed.

You will need to work on this. It is not easy, and it takes lots of work on your part. Let's look at it a little closer, so you understand where I'm coming from.

You must start with the first job that you have listed and outline all the sales-related activities that you performed in this job. (Be sure to use the past tense and present tense appropriately, depending on when skills were learned.)

A sales-related activity is defined as anything that involves prospecting, making phone calls, interacting with customers, reading emails, writing emails, answering calls, customer service, or any activity where you were working towards the goal of exchanging goods or services for money.

"But I didn't do any sales activities!!" Yes, you did. Everyone has performed sales-related activities at some point in their life. You will just have to dig deep and figure out how to articulate that the "stuff you did" was related to sales.

It's best practice to read that paragraph a couple of times and think about activities in your life that can relate. **A big part of**

this exercise involves creative thinking. If you have ever convinced someone to do something, you have performed a sales-related activity.

If you are a sales veteran, you want to make sure that your two-three bullet points highlight your sales-related activities in a measurable way. This will demonstrate that you can perform sales activities and that you have been held accountable to them in previous roles. This is important. It's not enough to just list your sales-related activities if you have already been in a sales role. This is because your activities are measured in a sales role. For instance, instead of putting down "met with five new prospects per week," … you would want to put "averaged five new prospects meetings per week against our team's mandate of three."

For beginners and seasoned reps, it's the same exercise with the only difference being that the seasoned reps will have measurable items included. You will notice that nothing so far has been related to achievement or quota. That is quite different compared to what everyone else tells you about how to build a sales resume. Let's dig into why I recommend activities over achievement.

Activities Over Achievement

All good sales managers want to understand if you can follow a sales process by actioning repeatable sales activities. **A good sales manager would rather see sales-related activities over**

quota attainment. Trust me. This is one of the biggest myths in sales. Here's why…

I cannot tell you how many times I have read a sales rep's resume, and their bullet points read something like this:

- Managed large enterprise accounts through territory organization while prospecting and negotiating with C-Level and C-Suite Executives

- Achieved quotas of 104%, 150%, 519%, 92%, 195%, and Club Excellence

None of this means anything to me. This would be the same thing as a Major League Baseball Player's resume stating:

- Played Major League Baseball against other professional athletes at some of the most prestigious stadiums around the country

- Won 88 games, 74 games, 90 games, and 92 games while making the All-Star Team

It might not make sense to you yet, so let me try to explain myself.

Your attainments and percentages are not as impactful as you might think. If you were a sales rep, this would be the same as if you sent out sales material that said, "Our company can increase 185% of revenue for you and save 10% in costs by delivering a great return on investment." The broad and generic messaging about ROI and percentages do not work in the real world, so why would they work on your resume? Some sales managers may fall for this tactic, but again, not the good ones—and those are the only ones you want to work for.

My entire goal is for you to demonstrate to a sales manager that you can follow a sales process. By calling out the actual sales-related activities instead of your performance against quota, you are demonstrating that you have followed a sales process before.

Here's a word problem to help you try to visualize what I'm saying.

If a sales rep achieves 235% of quota, and 230% of his quota came from an inbound partner-led deal, how much of his quota did he achieve? **The answer is 5%.**

The problem with listing all your amazing achievement percentages on your resume is that it does not demonstrate that you can follow a sales process. Achievement does not show action. Activities show Action! I know that some sales managers will say, "Well, if you are overachieving on your numbers, you must be capable of selling!" I beg to differ. That is not true at all. It is the biggest misconception during the sales job application process and could be preventing you from having a stronger resume

I knew a sales rep who woke up one morning, got his usual Starbucks order, and came into work just past 9 am. He sat down and began his usual routine of checking email. On that particular day, his inbox had a newly signed contract for $118k.

He screamed like he had just won the lottery. Let me break down what happened...

The night before, a prospect had gone to our website and downloaded the software that this guy was responsible for selling. The prospect then called our 1-800 number to let our call center know that he had downloaded the software. They sent him a contract, which he signed and scanned back to them. The call center automatically forwarded the email overnight to the sales rep's inbox while he was sleeping. A signed contract had been sitting in his inbox since 4 am and while he was getting his Starbucks that morning, he unknowingly had "sold" software.

In sales, we call this a bluebird. A bluebird is described as an easily completed and unexpected sale. This happens quite often at large corporations. Do you want to know the worst part? This rep's quarterly quota was $40k. So, on paper, he essentially achieved 295% of his quarterly quota! Such an achievement! What a great sales rep!!!

This rep now had the ability to include two new bullet points on his resume. One bullet would state "334% of quota," and the other would state "Q3 Sales Rep of the Quarter". At the time, I remember thinking, "He is going to have such a great resume now." I was young and naïve, but the truth is that a bad sales manager would love to hire him based on the achievements laid out in his bullet points.

However, if a good sales manager were interviewing him, they would be able to determine after some simple questioning that his attainment came from a bluebird.

I hope that you are no longer convinced that by listing your attainment, you're showcasing an ability to sell. If you are following my sales job application process correctly, you will need to put your ego aside here and try to break your bullet points out into purely sales-related activities.

For the veterans, if you want to include your achievement, I will show you where and how to do this later - even though it is not necessary.

Trust me. You are more likely to be invited in for an interview if you point out that you made forty to sixty cold calls per day with active follow-ups via email rather than pointing out that you hit 195% of quota.

Candidates always argue with me and stress that they want to show off their achievements and the Experience section is where experts say to do this. However, if that is best practice, then why do so many overachievers come to me for help with their resume? They come to me for help because they are not being invited to the interviews that they think they deserve.

If you are listing 285% of quota achievement as your only value-add at a company, you are not demonstrating how you got there or even that you know what kind of activities you should be doing to generate that kind of achievement. Maybe you got lucky? Maybe you had help? But a gold star on your resume does not demonstrate hard work nor sales ability.

If you are getting a lot of interviews with that type of information today, try to imagine how many more you would land if you demonstrated how you added value to your sales organization through action and activities.

This is a typical exercise that I will run through with candidates. It is focused on direct questioning that helps pull out the sales-related activities associated with each job or relative experience that you have had. After this exercise, you will be able to determine the different types of sales-related activities that you performed. Then you will be able to draft your bullet points accordingly, with plenty of sales-related activities.

Exercise 1: Prospecting Activities

Prospecting activities demonstrate you know how to engage potential new customers.

- Did you call people?
- Did you email people?
- Did you message people on LinkedIn?

Sample answer:

"I would call or email dozens of people a day based on who I found on LinkedIn."

Exercise 2: Accountability and Measurement Activities

Accountability shows the scope of your responsibilities, and measurement provides proof when you are asked to show evidence of your success.

- How often did you contact people?

- How did you measure it?

- Did a manager ask you how you were doing?

Sample answer:

"I typically made twenty phone calls a day and sent about ten emails. We kept track in Excel. I called low-level people that were given to us by a lead generation software."

Exercise 3: Sales Cycle Activities

These are the actions that show you know how to progress the sales cycle, make presentations, and handle objections.

- How did you advance conversations?

- Did you pitch someone?

- Did you provide a proposal or quote?

- Sample answer:

"We would try to confirm and set up phone meetings with the prospect and a sales rep. The sales rep would take it from there to discuss our product on the next call. We had a quota of thirty interactions per week."

Exercise 4: Closing Activities

This is any type of action you took to solidify the final step, handoff, follow up or close on your initial outreach.

- How did you confirm that a meeting counted against your goal?

- Did you confirm anything with a prospect?

- What happened next in your process (if anything)?

A call counted if we spoke to a prospect for more than 30 seconds. An interaction counted if we sent out the invite and it was accepted. Our manager asked us to achieve 100 phone calls, twenty interactions, and two meetings per week. I usually finished around 116.

Let's look at how you can craft your answers into three sales-related activity bullet points.

- Heavy prospecting (20 calls & 10 emails daily) with around 5-10 interactions fed by system-generated leads

- Set meetings with prospects for Sales Reps to progress cycles towards a demo and ultimately a proposal Measured weekly against 122 interactions, averaging 116.

The answers and the bullets will be different for everyone. These are hypothetical, but it is important that you understand the framework of my process.

Taking it one step further, let me show you how this exercise went for that client of mine who sold hot dogs at Fenway Park. If you are not familiar with this job, it's one where you wear a yellow shirt with a red apron full of cash while carrying a large hot dog oven over your head all summer long. Your job is to yell, "Hot dogs here!"

Let's look at some of his paraphrased answers to the questions above.

- I didn't call anyone. People just came up to me, or I walked by them in the park during the game, yelling out "Hot Dogs!"
- We would walk for about three hours during the game. The stadium held around 20,000 people. We were measured at the end of the game against how many dogs we started with and how many times we refilled our oven... Typically, I'd sell around 180-250 a game.
- Once a fan flagged us down, we would explain the price and then try to sell them more hot dogs. They could pay in cash or credit, but cash was easier for us.
- No measurement or quota, but I always kept track and usually sold more dogs than my friends.

Putting them into bullet points...

- Direct face to face interactions with upwards of 20,000 potential customers during a 4-hour baseball game for 82 days a year

- Face to face meetings with multiple prospects while trying to up-sell them on merchandise and encouraging them to make cash over card purchases

- Typically sold between over 250 hot dogs during each game, always finishing at the top of sales as measured nightly against my peers

I hope you can see what the goal is here. I am not asking you to lie, and I am not asking you to do anything crazy. The goal is for you to be able to transition the activities of <u>any</u> previous job that you have had into compelling sales-related activities.

After practicing these questions over and over, you should be able to adjust and readjust any job into a sales-related job. Start thinking of prospecting/interactions/customer-facing activities/measuring and accountability all the time when you think about the jobs you have had in the past. I have helped people from countless backgrounds identify sales-related activities after a bit of critical thinking.

After completing this exercise with your first job, this will become a repetitive exercise for each of the following jobs that you have had. Once you are done, your bullet points are finished. If you are still curious about what to do with sales awards or achievements, we will address that later.

Positivity

Unless you have had a flawless record since the dawn of time, there are always going to be negative things to address throughout a sales job application process. The best way to handle negativity is to wait for it to come up naturally and then counter with positivity and self-assurance.

We will never want to highlight a negative item upfront on your resume. This is why college students do not list below-average GPAs, nor should they. We also never want to bring up negative items in conversation. On both your resume and in conversation, you must lead with positivity and be ready to address a negative item if it comes up naturally.

Even if you had a bad boss or are leaving a terrible company, I encourage you never to lead with these topics. You will appear and sound desperate, and sales managers will notice. I have come across strong sales reps with low attainment just as often as I have come across weak sales reps with high attainment. So, if you didn't perform well, you don't have to beat yourself up over it and try to defend yourself immediately. Managers who sense negativity will only dig deeper. Shifting the blame or pointing fingers will always hurt your chances of proceeding.

It's best practice to see how far you can get before you start talking about a bad number or anything else that reflects poorly on you. You would never meet a guy at a bar and say, "Hi, I'm Meghan; I live at home with my parents because I just got divorced." This isn't how you lead if you're presenting yourself for the first time. I'm sure Meghan can think of hundreds of other better attributes to discuss when she meets a guy at the bar. She can talk about her divorce later and more strategically when it comes up.

Another common situation where candidates are quick to discuss things in a negative light is when they are discussing why they want to leave their current job. For some strange reason, candidates tend to be very negative when discussing their current role or situation, even if things are not that bad!

Candidates do this instinctively because they are trained that "current job bad, new job good."

A ton of candidates will bash or downplay their current role because they think that this is what sales managers want to hear. They think, "If I make it seem like a bad job with no room for growth or a stale culture, then they will understand why I'm leaving." Although this is very wrong, it is very common.

Your mindset throughout my process matters. You are essentially trying to sell yourself to other people. You are more marketable and more desirable as a candidate if you have a positive mindset. You must always convey to people that you are doing well in your current role and working for a company you respect.

Let's look at a real-world dating example.

Are you more interested in going on a date with Hugh or Tanner?

Tanner is open to dating someone if the timing is right. He spends his evenings training for a marathon and taking care of his new puppy. He is slow to respond to texts because he is usually busy. He is an avid sports fan and is trying to learn how to cook.

Hugh is open to dating anyone that wants to date him. He spends his time scanning dating apps for connections or messaging people on Facebook. He is available all the time and responds to texts immediately and just hoping to find someone to date soon.

Most people would want to date Tanner. Why? Because he is not desperate.

You should try to appear this way when you are looking for a job in sales. If you were a basketball coach, would you want to try to negotiate a trade for Lebron James, or would you try to trade for the next available player that wants to join your team? While most people answer Tanner and Lebron James, these same people act like they are desperate to leave their current company or current situation.

Why do we want to respond within 1 minute of receiving a recruiter's email? Why do we seem so willing to take any job? We do it because we are excited about the potential. I am telling you to act like you've been there. Make yourself desirable, and you will be desired. You should stand proud and hold high self-worth. It all starts with showing your current job in a positive light on your resume. If you downplay your current role on your resume, everyone will be able to sense your desperation.

When you start to put together the sales-related activities for your current role, you need to explain what you are doing and point out how it's been a positive experience. (Whether you have been promoted, taken on leadership roles, or gained any type of responsibility, it is best to highlight these things in a positive manner. If you point out how bad it is and that you want to leave, you will be dead in the water.

Once you have completed the bullet points for your current role, you are at the end of your experience. Your current role is where it ends for you, for now. When you can identify your past experience with sales-related activities and speak to your current role in a positive way, you will be shocked at how much more attracted sales managers are to you. More and more people throughout the process will want to meet with you.

I encourage you to try and talk through this section in thirty seconds or less. This will start to prepare you for how to tell your story out loud.

Smart people and good sales managers will be able to pick up your resume and learn your story within a minute. Trust me when I say that this is powerful. Sales managers do not want to read a novel, nor do they want to see mathematical equations related to quota. **When all is said and done, they just want to spend a minute reviewing your story.**

Education

Your Education section should be structured according to your age and career circumstances. I will make a few suggestions as to where I typically see candidates struggle the most, and this will provide you with a simple framework that you can build upon.

To begin, if you are a student or a recent graduate, it is best to position the Education section directly underneath your Summary. This will indicate to gatekeepers and sales managers that you are younger and at the forefront of your career. This will indicate that your university experience holds more relevance than your professional experience to date. This will allow you to cover up minimal job experience and utilize your Education as leverage.

For instance, if you are a senior at Holy Cross and you put your Education section at the bottom of your resume and instead decide to list a college dog walking job at the top, you are not leading with much of an impact. You are probably more involved in sales-related activities at Holy Cross than you are at walking dogs. Positioning your Education at the top will express have the potential to be coached by the right entry-level sales manager. It also will call attention to managers who are specifically looking for recent graduates.

A recent graduate is considered someone who was in college less than two years ago. After two years, you fall into the same category as the rest of us old people and should not include your Education at the top of the page.

We older folks should be putting the Education section at the bottom of our resume, underneath our Experience.

But what if I went to Harvard? I want to put it at the top! I hear this all the time. That's cool. Harvard is a great school. But you went there a long time ago. Don't lead with it. You can always bring it up later when you speak with someone. (Which I'm sure you will.)

Now that you understand where the Education section should appear let's look at how candidates mess it up. All you need to include is where you went to school, when you graduated and what you studied.

You don't need any more information. You can talk about other items later, but for now. it should appear like this...

University of Massachusetts - Boston, MA   May 2015

Bachelor of Arts in Philosophy

This format is acceptable for everyone to use. You never want more than this. Why? Because this is a sales job. It is not Academia, and it is not an industry where your education determines your sales ability

In fact, I have my MBA, and I have been in interviews where the sales manager asks, "An MBA?? Why'd you get that?" Salespeople do not care as much about education as you think. No one learns how to cold call at Stanford.

Avoid confusing your readers. I understand that it may be impressive if you are some sort of certified genius with a bunch of credentials and degrees, but I must stress that you are sending this resume out to gatekeepers and sales managers. I have seen an example like this before:

University of Worcester Polytechnic Sky Researcher's School (U of WPTISS)
Bachelors of Juniors Admin 1, C-Level 4 Extension program, on top of the roof, Honors
Curriculum 4,41.20 - X in Sociology
2010-2012 (then abroad a year 2013); 2013-2014 4pc

This would tip off any good sales manager that this candidate cannot summarize information properly. If a prospect were to ask them for information, they might send a four-page email with six attachments. Being a sales rep means you can summarize information for your prospects. Do not demonstrate otherwise on your resume.

A lot of serious academic people reading this book will argue, "But that is the official name of our school…and my degree is prestigious. Everyone will know what it means!"

Not everyone will know. I graduated from a great school in the US, and Canadians ask me, "What's Holy Cross? Is it a Priest school?" Even when I applied for a job in Florida, the head of HR asked me, "Is the University of Massachusetts an accredited college?"

Do not list out some convoluted name of an institution or program because you assume that most people should understand it because it is prestigious in your eyes. Your Education section is a small component of this powerful sales tool. You are using to get in the door. It is by no means an official document.

If you want to represent that previous example in a more sales-friendly manner, try something like this:

University of Worcester Poly - Worcester, MA	May 2014
Bachelors in Sociology, with Honors	

"Yeah, but you left out a ton of the good stuff!"

Good! You'll have plenty to talk about at the interview. No one wants to read that stuff, nor do they want to pass this kind of junk on to their head of sales. It is overwhelming. Your resume is a sales tool, not an encyclopedia. No one will ever tell you that too much detail is the reason why they aren't calling you. However, the reason they aren't calling you is that they're thinking, "this candidate can't summarize information... Let's find someone who can."

The general rule of thumb for your Education section is that less is more. If it was recent, put it at the top. If it was a while ago, put it at the bottom.

Awards

This is a tricky section for me. Most people tend to agree that a sales rep with a lot of awards must be a good thing, and those achievements should be acknowledged. Therefore, it makes perfect sense to list all your achievements on your resume.

I disagree. I worked in an office with hundreds of sales reps, and we all had our own cubicles. We would walk around and gather in each other's cubes to talk about deals, the weather, or the latest gossip. It was a little sales rep community. While in this community, I started to notice the cheap little crystal plaques that some reps placed on their desks. The plaques said things like, "MVP of The Quarter."

I noticed other reps with laminated pieces of paper that read, "Rep of the Month" or something like, "Top Closer Award." Other reps even had plastic "gold" trophies displayed

The reps who displayed such awards were always the "middle of the road" reps who had won an award once or twice. By displaying their achievements, they were trying to appear elite.

On the other hand, the best reps on the floor typically had things like a bowl of candy, family pictures, or an item they really cared about on their desk. These things opened up the door for a lot of conversation. One of the best reps at our company had a picture of Mount Everest on his desk. It was his life goal to climb it.

He won a ton of awards, and everyone knew he was one of the best reps on the floor. He did not have to display awards in his cube. The best reps never have to promote their "achievements" at work, and the same goes for your resume.

This is typically what candidates think looks good on a resume:

- 148% of quota in 2019 on a $1.85M annual target
- 124% of quota in 2018 Q1, President Circle Club for the quarter
- 230% of quota in 2016 Q2, President Circle Club Excellence for the quarter

While this may feel good to write out, I am critical, and if I were to analyze this information, my questions for the candidate would be as follows:

- What happened in 2017?
- What is the difference between those awards?

While achievement information may put you in the Elite category at your current company, it may open the door to a tough line of questioning from a good sales manager because most good sales managers are critical of data. It may also lead to a long and boring conversation about percentages.

People buy from people. They want to talk to you about life and other interesting things while they are buying from you. They don't care how much you've sold before. A good sales manager knows this and is looking for a sales candidate who is interesting and dynamic. They would much rather hire a sales rep who has great stories to share over the one with all the awards. Again, we discussed earlier that some of these 'achievements' could be connected to bluebirds too, so if the percentages are to be your main focus, you must ensure you can speak to each and every one in great detail.

If you feel confident speaking to your achievements, there is a way to include them all in a more approachable manner.

Using the achievements above, we can change the format to:

- Achieved over 100% for the past 3 out of 4 years, with multiple sales awards from senior leadership,

While this may seem a lot less powerful without actual numbers, any good sales manager will think, "Wow, this candidate achieved quota four years in a row. I need to interview them right away." Then, when you get to the interview, you can tell them about your 230% year. That will be the icing on the cake.

If you have been a high achiever, you are definitely good enough to not have to list every single percentage on your resume. Don't be the rep with your awards in your cubicle. Act like you've been there before and do it with a little bit of class. **If you have never received a sales award, there is no need to include an Awards section.** You'll get there one day. When you do, just remember to show a bit of humility, and it will go a long way.

Miscellaneous

Now, on to the "wild-wild-west." Honestly, an unstructured section like this is like giving a potential candidate a loaded gun. This section can be dangerous if you don't know what you are doing. Yet as dangerous as it may be, it is also an important section for candidates. When I am being interviewed, I find my Miscellaneous Section to be the section that leads to the best discussions. From the other side of the table, I often conduct my interviews based on items listed in a candidate's miscellaneous section. It is more conversational and fun… and conversations are a big part of sales.

Once, I interviewed a woman for a sales role who had listed that she had worked as a Clown selling balloons in the parking lot of a car dealership. We had a good laugh about it. It was great to hear her tell the story. I was able to gauge her storytelling abilities, her personality, and her motivation to sell. I eventually hired her because she was great at sales, and she also had a terrific sense of humor. Her customers loved her.

I will pause and say that I highly recommend running this section by a friend. I encourage you to run it by someone who will judge you. Do not run it by someone who will say, "Yes, that is good." Run it by someone who might say, "I'm not sure that is the best thing to put." Listen to these people, take their advice seriously, and then go ask a few other critical people. You will be judged on this section by gatekeepers and sales managers, so why not put it out there and ask to be judged beforehand? You just can't "wing" this section. The last thing I want is for every candidate to start writing down, "I used to be a clown" in this section.

For my Miscellaneous Section, I like to include the fact that I learned American Sign Language in college. That gets the right kind of attention and fosters a good conversation. Readers are instantly intrigued and want to know more about why I know ASL.

Unusual examples are not good to include here. Add something like a language that is relatable, rather than a topic that could be easily misconstrued. "Wide-Legged Belly Dancing" may draw the wrong type of attention... However, the fun and interesting things do work, and I encourage you to dig a bit and be vulnerable... just don't be *too* vulnerable.

Ask yourself, "What can I include here that will help my cause and not hurt me?"

Put acceptable hobbies or talents here. If you are thinking that it may be unrelated to sales, but it is something you do in your spare time, I encourage you to try including it. Some possible examples:

- Kettlebell Instructor

- Avid cyclist

- Irish Step Dancer

- Fundraiser for X organization

Don't overdo it, but take a shot and try to be bold. Gatekeepers and sales managers would love to have something interesting to talk to you about. Make yourself a bit more approachable, and don't take yourself too seriously.

This section may be very short for you and only be one or two bullet points. That is perfectly fine; just be careful not to overdo it.

Let me show you how to include something like a volunteer trip:

Volunteer Immersion Trip - Guatemala   June 2011
Renovated multiple homes with a team from NYC

This is the final product that I helped a candidate work into this section. She originally had it structured as follows:

Habitat4Humanity Session 3, Immersion Volunteer Sister/Brother Program
Guatemala for five months, Peru one month, and Rio for two months
Our team took flights down and built, renovated, updated multiple homes with a team from NYC, and we helped families with daily activities like drinking water and getting to work on time; it was really inspirational.

You must understand the difference between simply stating something on your resume to be talked about later versus trying to write down every piece of factual information so that it is "on the record." The more concise you are, the more conversations will open up.

Your job is to appear interesting with a small amount of information so that readers will want to invite you in to talk about it in detail. If you give them everything up front, they won't need to talk to you. They may even think that you lack summarizing skills. Good luck trying out different fun facts about your life and remember to run it by a critical friend.

Aesthetics

There are a few important aesthetic aspects to run through when it comes to your finalizing your Resume. If you are frustrated right now, I promise that we're almost done.

Please start by saving your resume as a PDF. This is to protect the file so no one else can improperly edit it when they open it. I have seen cases where a resume was sent as a Microsoft Word document, and a gatekeeper had deleted a few lines by accident. A PDF is the safest form and does not show red underlines, spelling mistakes, or blue underlines for grammatical mistakes.

Please also be cautious of the title of your document. I suggest saving your resume as "First Name Last Name Year." You don't need anything else.

I have received too many resumes titled " EXECUTIVE 11-2-451-CV2 J," and it is just distracting. It is a small aesthetic, but I encourage you to be less distracting, even with your file name. It goes a long way in sales.

For the rest of the document, I suggest keeping the color scheme in black and white with some type of standard, universally accepted font. Save the colors, pictures, borders, and other creative formatting for something else. Trust me; sales reps are often not artistic. Some of the best salespeople in the world need help to build a PowerPoint presentation. They barely know how to cut and paste. But these reps are very good at delivering information directly and concisely to prospects.

You may feel that you have an almost bare-bones resume, but I promise that you are going to be okay. Your new sales tool will open the door for many more conversations where you can talk and explain in detail about the items on there.

Every sales rep that I have ever met says, "I don't like a long PowerPoint with tons of text because it puts the prospect to sleep." Those same sales reps will send me their resumes with tons of text! I never understood this.

If you wouldn't show a busy PowerPoint when trying to pitch your product, why would you show a busy resume when trying to pitch yourself?

No one taught you that pitching yourself for an open sales job is exactly the process you go through when pitching a product to a prospect. There is a strong correlation between your resume and your sales presentations. Now that you have a resume that showcases the skills you bring to the table, you are ready to think about your brand.

John P. Davis

Toronto, Ontario

Email: davis.jpd@gmail.com   Phone: (647) 555-1234

Summary: Sales Rep looking to relocate to California in order to join a start-up sales organization. I am looking to learn from a sales leader who is ambitious and looking to scale the team.

Experience

ABC Company – New York City, US   May 2018 – Present
Sales Representative
- Daily prospecting involving 40-50 cold calls to prospects found on LinkedIn
- Set calendar meetings with prospects for Sales Reps to progress cycles towards a demo and ultimately a proposal
- Delivered proposals, quotes and business cases to decision makers

XYZ Solutions – Atlanta, US   2016 – May 2018
Inside Sales Representative
- Demand generation focused on emails and outbound messaging to prospects
- LinkedIn sequences aimed at 12-15 prospects per day with active follow up
- Measured against 222 interactions, averaging 216, with 4 meetings against our goal of 2

UMASS Sales Program – Dorchester, US   2015
Sales Intern
- Trained by Sales Reps and Sales Leaders in a well-known Sales Program

Awards

- Achieved over 100% quota from 2016-2018 with multiple sales awards
- Sales Rep of Q1 in 2016 at XYZ

Miscellaneous

- Volunteer Immersion – Peru   2011
  - Renovated multiple homes with group from NYC
- Kettlebell Instructor & Avid cyclist

Education

College of the Holy Cross – Worcester, US   2008
Bachelor of Economics

Your Story

Throughout your search for a new sales job, you're going to find yourself in several different situations where someone will ask about your experience or about how your search is going in general. This is very common, and if you don't have something put together, you will ramble on about things that don't matter. Candidates who have not formally put together a story will usually talk about generalities with all kinds of random facts thrown in.

It happens all the time. You meet someone at a party, and they ask, "Have you sold anything before?" Or maybe your cousin asks, "What kind of job are you looking for?" It will definitely come up in a formal sales interview.

In each situation, it is advantageous if you can effectively tell your story. How do you figure out what your story is? The good news is that we just built it together on paper. Your resume is a longer version of your story. It's your job to take this information and summarize it in your own words in 30 seconds or less.

This is difficult and will take some practice on your part. Your story is your elevator pitch on yourself. Don't spend all day telling it.

My guidance is to start with your education and move swiftly throughout your past jobs up until your current position while highlighting sales-related activities along the way. It should end very positively by including a bit of your summary (what you're looking to do next).

You don't have to repeat this verbatim each time you're asked about your job search or sales experience. Instead, I want you to think of it as a tool in your belt. We just put together your resume. This is your on-paper sales tool. Your story is your more versatile sales tool. You will be able to use it in emails, applications, interviews, cocktail hours, and whenever else you are trying to pitch yourself as a prospective sales rep. From here on, I will refer to your story throughout my process.

The greatest sales reps in the world are the ones who are the best at summarizing and storytelling. These top reps can summarize the livelihood of a deal and tell stories at will to captivate new prospects. By doing this on your resume and through other forms of communication, you will demonstrate an ability to summarize and to tell a story, captivating the attention of sales managers everywhere.

Learn your story. Practice it. Run it by a friend. Reach out to us at HowToGetASalesJob.com for more information on building an effective sales story.

You will find that having a compelling story about your experience is more powerful than general information regarding your employment. If done correctly, a sales manager will be able to quickly glance and understand where you're coming from.

Chapter 5: Branding

After completing your resume, you are still not ready to begin your official search for a sales job. We must first review your online presence and a few intangible soft skills to ensure you have a professional and approachable brand before reaching out to anyone.

Today, your entire life is only a few clicks away. The Internet is everyone's favorite research tool, and you must prepare to be judged before you even have a chance to speak with someone during your job search. Be aware that this type of online evaluation occurs during a sales job application process just as it would occur during any actual sales cycle.

If a sales rep were to hand you their business card at a party, there is a high probability you would look them up online before giving them a call. The same thing happens when applying to a sales job. Before you ever hear from a gatekeeper or sales manager, they will search for you on the Internet. More specifically, they will search for you on LinkedIn.

They will look you up to validate the information and to see if you have anything that disqualifies you immediately. It may seem judgmental, but this is the nature of sales. You must accept this fact and prepare accordingly.

Sales reps are judged on how they come across, how they present themselves, and their overall image. In order to be successful in sales, you must be approachable, likable, and professional. It is not important to have the looks of Tom Brady or the style of a Kardashian, but at the very least, you must appear sharp. If you messaged someone on LinkedIn and your profile picture was a blurry photo of you holding a beer, they are probably not going to respond. Their impression will be that you seem unprofessional, so why spend time or money with you.

This part of my process is identical to an actual sales process. Whether you are trying to sell a product or trying to land an interview, it makes no difference. Prospects and gatekeepers alike will look you up before making contact. We will ensure that your brand is bulletproof. This will mitigate your risk of being disqualified based on someone's initial observation.

We will focus our efforts on how to help you appear approachable, likable, and professional so that these "sneaky researchers" like what they see.

Google Your Online Brand

The first and most important thing you can do is to take an overall health-check of your current brand. To do this, you must find out for yourself what other people can learn about you online. This exercise will be eye-opening for some of you and scary for others. It is a critical first step in assessing and strengthening your online brand.

The first thing to do is to Google yourself. This may seem vain or superficial, but trust me… Google yourself. Go to Google, type in your name, and click search.

If you have a common name like me, you might be tough to find. However, a diligent person will try a few different ways of finding you. Try searching for your name and your hometown or university. This should return a few specific results on you. If nothing comes up after that, consider yourself lucky. You are done with this part. Most gatekeepers and prospects will stop after a couple of incomplete Google searches.

However, most of you will return results that contain links, images, or videos. It is up to you to ensure that they all work appropriately. If everything looks okay, you are also done with this part.

But what happens if you click search and find something inappropriate?

You should 100% try to remove that material.

I have worked with candidates who found their vulgar Tweets about an episode of "The Bachelor." Others found articles about traffic violations from when they were 17 years old. Things like this may not ruin your career, but they can certainly stop a gatekeeper cold in their tracks. There are plenty of other candidates without questionable search results.

In a split second, you are disqualified. Take time to research ways of deleting things from the Internet. It may require effort and even seem unimportant to you, but if you find something in your search that would make someone think twice, remove it. Please make every attempt to clean up your search results.

The worst part about not researching yourself is that you may never know that things like this exist. While you're fixated on perfecting your resume, sales managers might be disqualifying you because of that Halloween picture of you dressed as drunk Tinker Bell. As my good friend Oliver once said, "It's the things you don't know you don't know that should scare you the most."

In the rare case that something unsuitable is out there and cannot be deleted, you have three options. The first is to try to make contact with the site owner or hire an attorney (depending on the content). The second is to hope that no one Googles you. The final option is to talk your way out of it if it comes up. I recommend the first option. The best defense is a good offense in this situation.

If you don't remove material and are lucky enough that no one researches you, you are still on thin ice. You should take steps to remove this content because your future prospects will eventually find it, and it could prevent a sale later on.

If you find yourself having to address something like this, speak to it calmly and professionally. Remember our overview on positivity? If someone is willing to ask you about it, it may not be as detrimental as you might think. Therefore, address it as any professional would. The Internet has a lot of history, and it's okay to defend yourself as long as you are calm in the way you do it.

Social Media

Make sure your social media accounts are set to private. Please go ahead and take a minute to set your Twitter, Facebook, Instagram, Tik Tok, and your whateverelse.com to private. The only social media you want gatekeepers and sales managers to see is your LinkedIn. Everything else is a risk. I am not telling you to delete your social media accounts, but I am telling you to make them private during my sales job application process. If you want to make them publicly available after you land a sales job, go ahead. But during your search, it is important to set every account to private.

"But what if I have 100k followers on Twitter and I only post professional sales content?! Wouldn't they like this?"

I do not care about your followers or tweets, and neither will anyone in sales. If gatekeepers and sales managers really want to see your "professional sales content," they can friend request you. But by providing public access to your accounts, you are opening yourself up to unnecessary questioning. This can ultimately decrease the chances of moving forward in the process.

This example does not just relate to politics. Imagine if you post a ton of cat photos, and your sales manager is a dog person.

What if you always tweet about red and this manager likes blue? Regardless of whether you think this is fair, by allowing access to your social media, you are welcoming judgment from people. Social media is unnecessary while searching for a sales job. I want you to know that by allowing access, you are opening a door that doesn't need to be opened at this point.

LinkedIn

Next, you will want to spend some time updating your

LinkedIn profile. It is essential to have a professional and relevant LinkedIn. You do not need to be excessive, but you will need something that resonates with people's encounters in the wide world of sales.

People in sales take LinkedIn very seriously. Spelling mistakes, incorrect dates, or old profile pictures make two things very clear. First, you are demonstrating that you are lazy and out of touch with this amazing sales platform. Second, (and worse), you are demonstrating that you do not care about your image.

A gatekeeper or sales manager that sees your poorly set up LinkedIn will assume that you do not care about how you will appear to their prospects. This will hurt your ability to generate demand as a rep. A weak LinkedIn profile is a dreadful look if you are hoping to land a sales job.

The Basic "Must-Haves"

Making your LinkedIn profile sales-ready is not that hard. Let's take care of the easiest part first. Start by copying your job titles and company names directly from your freshly completed resume. Paste them in the same order into the appropriate fields on LinkedIn. If you ensure that these items are all correctly aligned with your resume, you are done with this part.

You do not need to include the bullet points that explain the sales-related activities you performed at each job. This is overkill for LinkedIn. Your profile is meant to be an even more abbreviated version of your resume, so it is acceptable to have less material. It is also a public platform, so you do not need to share these items with your entire network. They are only intended for hiring managers and are considered excessive for a LinkedIn audience.

You do not need to list anything more related to your work experience than what I have already mentioned. It may feel like a skeleton profile right now, and that's okay. Anything else is just fluff. Fluff is not a differentiator, and it can hurt you by inviting unnecessary questions. If your profile is tight, you will be judged a lot less when gatekeepers are doing their research. During my process and during an actual sales cycle, being judged less by prospects is always a good thing.

Titles and Acronyms

How often do you see a profile name like **Joe Smith, MBA** or **Caitlin Stevenson, CPA, PMP**? Quite often. LinkedIn has given people the ability to see other people's brands, which leads to conformity. Candidates see a profile with something interesting or with a certain buzz word and think, "I should do that too!"

The type of candidates that include acronyms after their name will typically follow with a summary that states, "After achieving my MBA…" or "Chartered Professional Accountant with a Project Management Professional certification…" The mentions of degrees and certifications continue down the page in other sections. It's repetitive (and redundant). It is perfectly fine to be proud of these achievements.

However, by highlighting these designations in your name and in other parts of your profile, sales managers without that type of degree might be rolling their eyes. In sales, these items don't carry as much weight as in other professions. This is a hard pill to swallow, but it can be a point of contention.

Only include acronyms after your name if you would greet someone new by saying, "Hi, my name is Joe Smith, MBA." No? You don't do this? No one talks like this, and you shouldn't either. Jamie Dimon does not list himself on LinkedIn as Jamie Dimon, MBA. He is the CEO of JP Morgan and has earned an MBA, but it is not part of his name. You can include your acronyms in your Education section, but let's agree that in sales, your name should have no capitalized letters after it.

Headline

Another small but somewhat important piece to consider is your headline. LinkedIn requires you to include a headline on your profile. This is a one-liner that appears in Italics under your name when people search for you.

A headline is defined as a catchphrase or slogan. The most famous in the world is Nike's "Just Do It." I do not have a slogan as good as Nike's (no one does) but mine is short, and it works for me. I use "Sales at OneStream," which is what I currently do.

When someone looks me up on LinkedIn, they will instantly see in my headline and know that I am in sales. This is much better than leaving people guessing what I do or what my intentions are professionally. You are in the process of applying for a sales job. You want people to know you're in sales in some capacity. Tell them this in your headline – just keep it short.

Most people, even some of my best friends, write out long sentences for their headline. I see so many that say, "Helping and coordinating with organizations to better remedy their optimal process..." Gatekeepers and sales managers will only be able to see a cut off version when searching for you. They'll see, "Helping and ..."

I would estimate that 95% of sales candidates on LinkedIn have an overbearing headline. This will hurt you because people may not recognize right away that you are in sales. Or worse, they will think that you're in some other line of business, therefore not qualified. Most candidates do not realize this is an issue because they've never been told.

The headline is just another minor detail that is often missed and can be cause for someone to pass on you. As a sales manager, if I see that someone overlooks details repeatedly throughout the job application process, I am less inclined to interview them. I am not saying this one detail would stop me, but it can definitely add to a growing list of misses

Nike – "A sportswear company and athletic apparel shop that focuses on……."

Nike - "Just do it."

You tell me which one is a better headline.

Profile Picture

A lot of candidates struggle with posting a proper profile picture. At first, I missed this as well because I was intimidated by the thought of taking a professional photo. I also do not like taking any type of photo. But it is no excuse. We will review a couple of options to show you what type of photo is acceptable in sales.

First off, make sure your picture is recent. A lot of people will use an old picture, but this can be misleading when you meet in person. If your profile picture is ten years old and you are meeting a manager for the first time in person, their initial thought might be, "Wow, they do not look anything like their profile picture. That's strange…." If you think this is just a quick and impulsive thought, you are wrong. Someone's first thought is important. If they are wondering why your picture was old, they will not be as focused on you as a candidate. To avoid this type of awkward encounter, use a current photo. I consider a current photo to be within one to three years old at most.

If you can afford professional pictures and you have time in your day to take them, then you should go and do that. Just make sure that you are wearing something comfortable that you look good in. Do not wear a big baggy suit just because you think wearing a suit is what people want to see. **Wear something that makes you look and feel confident**. Ask a close friend if you have issues with your appearance but make sure that your friend is honest. You do not want bad advice. It is better to look good in a more casual outfit than it is to look bad in formal attire.

If you cannot get professional photos, you can use a smartphone. Try to use a new phone with a solid camera. You want it to be a clear image. Have someone take a few pictures of your face up against a white wall in the outfit that you feel most confident in.

Make sure your picture is well-lit and that you are smiling. You do not need a big toothy grin, but you want to ensure that your mouth is in the form of a smile. Gatekeepers, sales managers, and prospects alike will mentally decide if they should meet with you based on your profile picture. It is human nature that **people are more inclined to meet with someone who is smiling.** It is the most appealing thing that you can do in a photograph.

You may have to ask a few friends or family what they think about your picture before posting it on LinkedIn. Choose a recent, well-lit photo that shows confidence and a nice smile, and you will nail it. This type of picture will demonstrate that you are a professional salesperson, and believe it or not, a smile will sometimes separate you from the pack.

Cover Image

Behind your profile picture is a cover image. Candidates will traditionally use a company logo or city skyline here. These are both perfectly acceptable and fine to use these types of images. Keep it simple, and do not make it too distracting. Some candidates have inspirational quotes or other motivating images. Your cover photo can tell a little bit about you in a subtle way. I use a picture of outer space as mine. I used to use my company logo but then realized I would have to change it whenever I joined a new company. Have a bit of fun with this—just don't distract from the fact that you want a professional sales job. Try not to leave it blank.

Summary & Education

Your summary and education on LinkedIn are straightforward. You can literally copy and paste these items from your resume as you see fit. You may have to lightly edit your summary for LinkedIn if the one you used on your resume is focused on a specific job. For example, you don't want your summary on LinkedIn to be geared towards a pharmaceutical sales role. LinkedIn is a much broader audience. Your summary here should be generalized.

For your Education, you only need the name of the University and the degree that you received. Less is more on LinkedIn when it comes to education. For salespeople, it is a reference point, not a talent show.

Once you finalize your Education section, you are done with your profile. When applying for a sales job, you do not need anything else on your LinkedIn page.

If you want to be a bit fancier, or if you are very comfortable on LinkedIn, you can join some groups, follow sales leaders, add some interests, etc. There is no harm in doing this at all. But for the bare-bones requirements when it comes to getting a sales job, you just need to just nail the items I have laid out.

I am not trying to coach an army of sales reps to have standard LinkedIn profiles. Rather, I want you to understand that while searching for a new sales job, it is better to tighten up your online brand. You will be less exposed and face fewer objections, questions, and hesitations from gatekeepers.

Once you have created a solid LinkedIn, checked that you have no dirt on Google, and set your social media accounts to private, you have succeeded in creating a strong online brand.

 We are not entirely done with branding. Part of your brand as a sales rep will be based on how you communicate with others. If your communication style comes off as unpolished, you might find yourself in a bit of trouble. It's time for a quick refresher to polish your phone and email skills before we sign off on your overall sales brand.

Phone Skills & Etiquette

The two most important parts of a phone call in sales are the beginning and the end. Whether you have never used the phone, or you use it quite often, my process will provide you with the necessary framework to ace a sales call. By demonstrating strong phone skills, sales managers everywhere will be keen to invite you in for an interview. Let's start by looking at how to answer your phone.

Greeting

"Hello....?"

This is how most candidates answer the phone when I call them. The way they ask "Hello," so casually, makes them sound like they are lost or confused. It reminds me of the scene in *Home Alone* where Macaulay Culkin is walking around his house, calling out, "Hello....?" when he first realizes that his family left him.

Other times when I call people, they pick up and say something like, "Hey John." Both greetings are entirely acceptable if you are part of the general public. **However, you are no longer considered a part of the general public. You are now part of the sales world.** In sales, your phone etiquette is vital to your success. Normal human beings may not notice nor care how you sound on the phone, but a sales manager is going to jump on it right away. It is important to be ready to rock on the phone.

I learned the importance of phone skills from a British colleague of mine named Courtney. No matter what, he would always answer his phone like this:

Before 12 pm: Good morning; thank you for calling Deutsche Bank. This is Courtney speaking; how can I help you?

If it were after 12pm, he changed 'morning' to afternoon, and if it were after 5 pm, he changed 'afternoon' to 'evening.' The rest of the greeting remained constant.

He was always warm and welcoming, even though we worked in a high-stress environment. Even when expecting an angry hedge fund manager, Courtney would take a deep breath and answer his phone with this greeting and a smile. Why? Because he understood that we were in sales.

I asked for his feedback on my calls. I usually answered with, "John speaking." Courtney told me that it was "fine" but that I sounded "a bit cold and abrupt." Here I am listening to how pleasant my co-worker sounds, and I did not once consider what I sounded like. It became clear to me that I needed to change my approach.

I took his advice but made his greeting into my own. I was from Massachusetts, and his friendly English greeting was too long-winded for me. Over time, I developed what is my "best practice" for greeting anyone on the phone in sales.

"Good morning, this is John speaking." Trust me. This will be very difficult for most of you. When I first tried it out, it sounded like I was putting on an acting voice. It was tough to get the words out, and I said it softly because I thought it sounded lame. However, over the years, it has helped me to have a very strong and positive start to sales calls.

Take a second and practice your greetings right now. Look at your clock and determine which greeting you should use. Repeat it a couple of times out loud. Learn to love it. This is how professional sales reps answer the phone.

If it is Friday night at midnight and your phone shows that your best friend is calling, you don't have to greet them like this. If you have scheduled a phone interview at 3 pm with a sales manager named Katie and you are sitting there expecting her call, I still encourage you to use my greeting. Don't assume anything or try anything outside of my process. In this scenario, by using my greeting, there are a few things that can play out.

Katie will appreciate your polite greeting. You will not creep her out. It will appear as though you were busy working and not just sitting by the phone. Or if it's someone else calling on Katie's behalf, you won't have to explain yourself or start the conversation on the wrong foot.

How you greet someone when you pick up your phone is especially important in sales. It is the most fundamental issue that I come across when working with candidates. Imagine how you want to make prospects feel when they call you. Your greeting is not only a representation of yourself but also of your company. Too many candidates take how they sound on the phone for granted.

Think about how you are greeted at Subway versus how you are greeted at The Ritz Carlton. At The Ritz Carlton, the front desk smiles and greets you politely by name. At Subway, they might barely look up from the counter and mutter an obligatory, "Hi." Your brand in sales does not start and stop online. It permeates through into how you handle yourself on the phone as well.

You can learn a lot from how people speak on the phone, and I encourage you to start thinking about it more. Try listening to others around you, and you will soon begin to hear who sounds good and who sounds bad. Salespeople are great at speaking on the phone. It is a craft that you should always continue to develop.

Throughout my process, you are going to interact with a lot of new people, and you are going to take calls from a lot of people in sales. You want to make people immediately feel comfortable with you and feel a welcoming presence. It will go a long way, trust me. Try to work on it.

When you are calling someone versus answering your phone, it is very straightforward. When you are making a call, always start with, "Hi Ashley, this is John Davis, how are you? Regardless of how someone answers your call, I recommend starting the conversation this way. This leads us to our next topic – what to say when someone asks, "How are you?"

How Are You?

According to my high school English teacher, the best response is that you are "doing well". It is grammatically correct. But in all honesty, you do not have to focus on which adjective to use. I usually say, "Good, thanks, how are you?" I have had Senior Executives coach me to say, "Fantastic" or "Terrific" because it elevates the tone of the conversation. Other people have advised against saying "good" because it makes you sound ignorant. So, what should you say?

If someone is a stickler about how you respond to this question, you probably do not want to work for them. All you need to do is make sure that you are authentic and that you *are* genuinely interested in how the other person is doing. They will be able to sense your interest. Do not try to be someone else, and do not try to talk like your grammar teacher. There is no right answer to how you respond, but I wanted to point this out because it comes up a lot. If you are openly engaged, you should have no problem.

Being engaged means that you are paying attention to the conversation. If someone replies and tells you that they are "doing okay, I guess," it might be a good idea to ask them if everything is okay. Not only will it show that you care, but it also shows that you are aware.

Sometimes you might ask a sales manager if everything is okay, and they will tell you, "Actually, no. My VP just emailed me about my forecast, and I have to get this submitted. Can I call you back in an hour?" This could happen, and it is good for you to be aware of how they're doing at the beginning of the call. The last thing you want to do is to have a twenty-minute conversation while the other person is not paying attention. You will most likely not leave an impact.

Pay Attention & Other Tips

When you are on the phone, please shut your laptop. Do not look at websites or emails while talking to someone on the phone. Do not watch TV. When your mind subconsciously wanders away from the phone call, a smart person on the other line will be able to sense you are distracted. I can sense it. I used to make over 100 phone calls a day, and I knew when someone was doing something else while on the line with me. To this day, I can still make a very strong guess as to what people are doing when I am speaking with them. It is critical to pay attention to the conversation and not to do two things at once.

Don't talk on the phone while you are sitting down. Stand up and look out a window or walk around the room. Try it right now. Go sit on the couch and say, "Good morning, this is John Davis speaking."

Now stand up and say it. You should feel a difference in your diaphragm and how you are projecting. You do not need to yell or purposely be loud, but you do need to stand up.

Some candidates use the speakerphone as a way of sounding important, but I have found this to be problematic. With speakerphone, I cannot assume or trust that the person on the other line is alone. On those occasions, I will not feel free to speak my mind. It is an inconsiderate way to use your phone, especially in a one-on-one conversation. I advise against it.

If you happen to be on a call that enables other people to potentially hear the conversation, let your caller know that they are on speakerphone but that you are alone. If the caller must ask you why you are on speakerphone, you have already lost a step in the conversation by not being upfront about your situation. Simply say, "By the way, Lisa, I am in my car, and you are on Bluetooth, but I am alone. I just wanted to give you a heads up." Lisa's skepticism is gone, and the conversation keeps moving.

Interruptions

Something may happen in the background that will affect the conversation. Interruptions happen all the time and they are impossible to plan for. For example, you could be in a quiet coffee shop in your hometown, and the fire alarm goes off. Or you could be upstairs in your home office, and someone rings the doorbell. I have heard all kinds of stories from candidates related to interruptions.

No one can control everything around them. Yet, it is important to try to mitigate some of the most common interruptions that can occur. For instance, don't take a call while you are boarding an elevator. Or do not take a call while your plane is about to take off. Try to be somewhere quiet when taking a call, especially if you are expecting one.

Acknowledge an interruption when it occurs. This is the polite way of showing the person on the other line that you respect their time and conversation. It is acceptable and beneficial to let the person know what is going on around you and what you are going to do to fix it. Sometimes even ending the call is best.

I am perfectly fine with someone telling me, "Oh, John, I am sorry. The fire alarm in my building is going off. Can I please mute you for a minute?" That shows me professional courtesy because what they are saying is true and polite. It is bad manners to ignore the alarm or to laugh about it and wait for it to stop. You must address it directly; otherwise, the caller will be left wondering about your etiquette when you are speaking with a prospect.

If you do not acknowledge an interruption, it can appear rude and may also be uncomfortable for the person on the other line. This has the potential to ruin your phone call and your candidacy. This is especially important to understand because, throughout my process, most of your phone calls are going to be planned. This gives you a lot of control regarding your environment, and if you run a planned call poorly, you will ruin your chances of moving forward.

Don't Be Late

It may be acceptable to be a minute or two late to a phone call in other areas of your life, but when it comes to sales, you cannot be late to a phone call. It is a sign of disrespect and a sign of poor time management. If you dial-in late to a phone call during a sales job application process, you run the highest risk of not moving forward.

The main reason is that the person on the other line will assume through your actions that you will also be late to calls with prospects. If you are late to prospect calls, it will reflect poorly on you, your company, and the sales manager who hired you. They cannot afford to hire a rep who cannot do something as simple as being on time. It can stop you dead in your tracks. I have seen it happen.

I coach candidates to be ready early. Whether you are calling the sales manager, dialing in to a conference line, or waiting for a call, be sure that you are ready at least two minutes early. Being ready one minute before the agreed-upon time can sometimes cause tardiness.

The reason that I suggest being ready at least two minutes early is because of things like a busy signal, wrong number, or even if the clock you are looking at is off by a minute. These things happen, and when a candidate is late, they always start the conversation with an extensive explanation of what happened. Rather than managing the time properly and having a strong start, candidates will open with: "Hey John, sorry, I am late. I had an issue with my phone."

This is a bad way to start a phone call in sales. By explaining why you're late, it makes you look weak. It is not the excuses nor the apologies, though. It is the plain and simple fact that you cannot manage time well enough to be on time. Sales managers are looking for reps who can follow a process. If you cannot manage your time appropriately, you will be able to manage an entire sales process.

Calling someone early is acceptable. If someone called me three minutes early, the conversation is one hundred times better than if they had been one minute late. When someone is early, this is usually what happens…

"Hey John, It's Kevin. I know I am a little early, but I was wondering if you had time now to chat."

"Hi Kevin, thanks for calling, sure this works."

Or worst case, "Hi Kevin, actually, yes. Can you give me five minutes and call me back? I am just about to grab a coffee."

In both scenarios, you are golden. You have checked the box off that shows you pay attention to time management. In the scenario where I was grabbing a coffee, that is fine too, because I know that Kevin understands the importance of being on time. It is not a bad thing to be early for a phone call, but it is <u>game over</u> if you are late. Make sure you have the right phone number, the correct time, and are ready early. You should do the same with your prospects after you have landed the sales job.

E-mail & Other Messaging

Over 200 years ago, Edward Bulwer-Lytton wrote, "The pen is mightier than the sword." I am not sure if Edward was in sales, but boy, was he right. In sales, more than any other profession (except for maybe journalism), you will live and die by your messaging. Your brand is incomplete until you review your messaging etiquette. In 2020, most of the world assumes that they understand the dos and don'ts of e-mails, texts, and other forms of written communication. However, there are still many easily avoided mistakes made during a sales job application process. I will share the best practices so that you know how to message properly and what to avoid.

You must demonstrate that you are a professional sales rep who understands how to communicate appropriately. You are going to have a lot of messaging interactions with people, and it is important to sound and look the part. It isn't easy, so let's start by taking a closer look at the many different forms of messaging and how you can employ them.

Messages: Many Types, One Goal

Most of your correspondence throughout this process will be via e-mail or LinkedIn messages. There are odd instances where texting may occur, but I'd advise you to use e-mail or LinkedIn over texting as much as possible. This will help you avoid any type of accidental or inappropriate texting. E-mail is the best form because it is the most official and usually a good sign that they are taking you seriously.

The goal of any correspondence during my process is to move the ball forward. This typically happens by outlining a situation and then identifying and asking for a next step from the reader. If any of your messaging does not address the current situation and identify the next step, it will fall flat, and you will be left hanging. This is also true in an actual sales cycle.

Have you ever sent an email and not received a response? There are certainly those one-off situations where someone might purposely ignore you, but a lack of response usually occurs because you are not asking the reader for a next step. Your reader will glance over your e-mail and not respond because it does not require any action from their end. If you *did* ask for a next step and still did not get a response, it is perfectly acceptable to reach out again. In your next message, identify that you had asked the reader for action regarding the next steps and that you are still interested in hearing from them.

If your first email did not ask for a next step, and your second email asks for a next step, all you did was waste time between those two emails. Time is especially valuable in sales and throughout a sales job application process. Your messaging needs to be structured efficiently so that you do not waste your time or the reader's time. Summarizing a situation and asking for action is the best way to save time and generate the need for a response.

Don't Just Fire Off Messages

When you first decide that you want a sales job, it is a natural tendency to begin reaching out to your family, friends, and former colleagues to see if they can help. I am going to address ideal contact methods in my section on Targeted Networking, but I want to outline best practices here so that you are more aware when you get excited and start thinking about corresponding with others.

Here is a scenario that might resonate. Your best friend works in sales at Google, and you have heard she is crushing it. Maybe she has inspired you, and this is the reason why you want to get into sales. In this scenario, most candidates will start their search by immediately shooting off a careless text to their friend at Google.

```
Hey girl. I am thinking of getting into
sales. How's Google? Are you guys hiring? lol
```

This literally happens all the time. It still happens to me on a regular basis. I did this when I was first trying to get a sales job, and I did not realize how badly it played towards my brand. How bad can an innocent text like that be, especially if it is a close friend or relative?

The first problem is that you are diminishing the importance of that person's job. You are making it seem like you can easily get a sales position at Google by sending a casual text. This makes it seem like you think you can switch over into a sales job at Google that might have taken your friend many years of hard work to achieve. The recipient of this text will think that you must not be too serious. The most common response will be, "We aren't hiring now, but let me know if you want to talk about this in the future."

This response is your friend's indirect way of saying, "Get your act together. This is Google, and we aren't just hiring my friends that text me. What's your resume look like, and why are you looking to get into sales?"

While no one in their right mind would send you this type of formal response back over text, it is what they're thinking. Texting is limited and informal in nature. It downplays the significance of your message and may suggest you are insincere. It's not the best way to communicate with anyone throughout my process. Even if the person is your best friend since second grade, I do not recommend texting them.

The tone suddenly changes if you were to send that same friend a slightly more formal message on LinkedIn or via email. I understand that it may seem awkward to message your best friend this way, but in the world of sales, this will feel like second nature for them. They will not think twice. If they give you a hard time for not texting, just explain that you wanted to be more formal than usual and that you are trying to figure out this whole sales thing. They will laugh but appreciate and understand your approach.

Rather than a text, try sending your friend at Google an email that looks something like this.

"Hi Amanda, I wanted to see if you were open to catch up after work next week. I am trying to revamp my career and find a sales role. I saw that Google has a Sales Rep III Role in London on their site. The job code is 401088RRF. I know that you have been there for a while, and I wanted to pick your brain on the job, culture, etc. Let me know if you are open to discussing and when would be best for you."

You have clearly identified the situation by stating that you are looking to find a sales role, and you saw that Google has an opening. You asked for potential next steps: your friend must pick a date that works to connect. It is simple and direct. This is the type of messaging that you must start familiarizing yourself with if you are going to be in sales.

Many candidates will ask me questions like, "But what if there are no open jobs at Google?" Others will argue, "I don't want that specific job." Or maybe even something like, "I just want to ask her for a date and time and not about a particular job yet." All of these are valid questions, but I am telling you as best practice what works. If you do not want to include job titles, locations, or anything specific, that is your call. My process provides you with the most effective way to open a line of communication with someone while looking for a sales job. You must understand that it is important to keep it somewhat formal (even with friends and family) and always ask for concrete next steps.

This type of messaging will instantly legitimize your candidacy as a potential sales rep at Google. You demonstrated that you could describe a situation and request the next steps. Even if you don't want that specific job at Google, or even if it is the wrong location, it still shows you understand the basics of sales messaging when reaching out. It also shows professionalism and ambition. You will be way ahead of the fifteen other people who texted your friend Amanda and said, "Hey, how's Google these days?"

By using my suggested messaging etiquette, most of the network will respond with something like, "Hi John, that is actually not the role you want, but I can connect you with someone who is hiring." Or they will come back with, "What is up with the formal email? Funny that you reached out, though. We are killing it, and I can talk to you more about it next week. Call me Tuesday."

Bingo. Either way, you are moving the ball forward. If you sent that lazy text, you would have gotten a lazy response. Try using more professional messaging. It will reflect very well on your brand. You may get a hard time from your closest friends for being too formal, but I promise you that they will be more inclined to help you out.

Cold Messaging

Texting someone you do not know is a nonstarter. That is stalker behavior, and I do not advise you to try it. If you cannot text a stranger, what is the etiquette when reaching out? Do you use the same type of messaging that you used with your family or friends? The answer here is… kind of.

When you are messaging someone you do not know, the best way to do this is via email. If you do not know the person's email, the next best thing to do is to message them on LinkedIn. With either platform, you can mimic the messaging structure that you used with your friend, <u>but you must add another layer of caution and formality</u>. You must be overly sensitive and professional when messaging someone you have never met before because you are uncertain of who they are or how they will react.

For instance, you may believe that you are messaging a 31-year-old Human Resources Analyst on LinkedIn. But in reality, that person has not updated their LinkedIn profile in fifteen years, and you are really messaging the 46-year-old Chief Human Resources Officer who is in charge of hiring for the entire organization. If you took the casual approach because you thought it was "just an HR analyst," you might be in for a rude awakening when you realize that your casual email just went to the CHRO.

> 'Hi Steve, I am interested in discussing your opening for [POSITION] at [HIRING COMPANY]. I am available at times listed below and have attached my resume for your reference.
>
> >   Thursday: 10am-1pm
> >   Friday: 11am-4:30pm
>
> Please let me know if you have 30 mins and I will send over a calendar invitation for a call.
>
> Best,
>
> John

If your cold messages are too long, they will go unread. If they do not ask anything of the reader, they will not generate a response. It is a step up from the formality used with someone you already know, but you have still summarized your intent and requested the next steps. Adding anything additional just opens up unnecessary questioning.

Here is a professional tip for generating more responses to your cold messaging. People are busy. They do not know you. They are not going to interrupt their already full calendars to accommodate your request. I have learned this technique from many years in sales, and I use it to guide the reader towards the next opening on their calendar. Offer dates that are most likely to get you a "Yes" answer.

If you are sending a cold message to someone in the first half of the week (Monday-Wednesday), it is best to suggest dates for the call to happen later in the following week. Alternatively, if you are sending a cold message to someone late in the week

(Thursday or Friday), you will want to suggest a couple of days early in the week after next. Both of my suggestions will seem very far away, so why do it this way?

Most candidates will request a call on the same day or the very next day. That is crazy to me! Who has time to drop everything and take a call right away with a stranger? Regardless of who you're reaching out to, 99.99% of people will not be able to put a new call on their calendar the same day or 48–72 hours out.

The reason I coach candidates to ask for 72+ hours out is that it is psychology. Most salespeople's calendars are full for up to 72 hours. A lot of new people in sales (even some veterans) still email sales managers or SVPs of sales and ask for a call within 48 hours.

If you ask for an appointment time 72+ hours out, you are more likely to get a response. Trust me; you can wait a few extra days for the meeting. There is no legitimate reason to ever ask someone you do not know for a meeting on the same day or the next day. It is way too invasive.

Also, you will be surprised how many sales professionals book meetings two weeks out. You will see results, I promise.

A second pro tip on cold messaging: if the person's response is, "Yes. I can give you thirty minutes on Friday at 6 pm." <u>You must take that call.</u> Unless you have a life or death situation that is more important than getting a sales job, you are on the hook to make that time work. It may sound aggressive, but there aren't many things that should come in the way of this initial call. **You are asking someone for their time.** If they are kind enough to provide you with an opening on their calendar, <u>take it.</u>

When I was a sales manager, I had situations where I would respond to a candidate: "I am swamped, but I can give you thirty minutes at 7:45 am next Tuesday." This was legitimately the next open slot on my calendar that I could offer them. Yet nine times out of ten, my offer would be met with, "I cannot make it at that time. Can we do 10 am instead?" After an exchange like that, I usually end my correspondence with them.

I opened their cold email and offered the next available time in my calendar, and they still turned me down. This was my first impression of them. They declined a meeting without reason and lazily proposed a new time in the middle of the day. Potentially, I was going to be their future boss. If I hired them and they did this to one of our prospects, I would be very disappointed. Imagine reaching out to the SVP of Media at Disney and then switching the time on them to benefit your schedule.

If a person responds with a time and you absolutely cannot make it work, there is a proper way to handle it. Keep in mind; your excuses should only be things like funerals, flights, car accidents, or deaths. Be truthful and direct. Lying is the worst. If you have to meet your friend at a bar or have a CrossFit class, you will be judged accordingly. You also need to re-evaluate your priorities.

However, if you do have a dire circumstance that will cause you to miss the proposed time, I suggest something like this, "Hi Joe, I cannot make it Friday at 6 pm because I will be at my daughter's play that I committed to months ago. The play gets out at 8:30 pm, I can either make a call then, or perhaps we can do another time you are free, and I'll adjust my calendar."

This is the only proper way to decline someone who has offered you a time slot. You must offer a valid reason and suggest a time <u>immediately after</u> when you are open. Then you must follow that up by suggesting that you are free any other time besides 6 pm on Friday. This is not the best option, but it is the only way to decline if you absolutely must.

If they *do* accept your response and provide you with another time to talk the following week, you <u>cannot</u> miss the new proposed time. If you miss their second suggestion, it is time to hang up your cleats. You are probably not cut out for the job, and you are probably not cut out to be in sales. If you like more information on messaging check out HowToGetASalesJob.com

Now that you understand the general approach to messaging acquaintances and cold contacts. Once you first realize that you want to get into sales, you can see why it is important not to jump right in. In the next section, we are going to dive deep into the art of using e-mail and LinkedIn messaging effectively.

I have included this overview of phone and email etiquette because there may be cases where you need to communicate with someone early in the process. Perhaps you met someone at a bar, and they told you to email them, or maybe your neighbor just posted on LinkedIn about hiring a sales rep at her company. If you find yourself in a situation where you need to act fast, or if you are already involved in communications about a job, at least you will understand the basics. Your communication reflects your ability to handle sales.

Phone and email etiquette are an integral part of your brand. I don't want you to appear as though you are part of the general public any longer. Your brand really does matter in sales, so it is important to address this upfront in case it comes up naturally.

Try to hold off on a lot of messaging for now, but just understand that any initial communication reflects on your brand just as much as Internet research.

John P. Davis

Chapter 6: Targeted Networking

A fter preparing your sales material and refreshing your brand, you are now ready to begin contacting people to let them know you are in the market for a new sales job. Where do you start? Before a sales rep begins reaching out to prospects, they are given a list of accounts from their manager. Without a list of accounts, sales reps are not able to plan out their territory approach accordingly. They are left helpless.

In a sales job application process, no one will give you a list of target accounts. It is entirely up to you to build a list of target companies. To take it a step further, no one will even tell you how to come up with such a list. How do you know what to look for?

Together we will build a target list of companies where you want to work. We will segment, prioritize, and categorize companies based on your needs and wants. Once you feel good about your list, I will provide you with the best practices on how to approach, contact, and network with employees at your targets. It must be done in a way that continually demonstrates you understand the importance of a sales rep approach with prospects.

When we combine your targets, your approach, and your contact methods into one, we are complete the section of my process known as Targeted Networking. Before we begin making a list of targets, it's very important to reflect on how important your overall approach will be in a sales job application process.

Why Focus on Approach?

Most people believe that a sales rep from Microsoft has a hard time losing a deal to a competitor with an inferior product. That is simply not true. Microsoft sales reps lose deals quite often. When this happens, the rep typically blames the loss on something like price, timing, or lack of budget. However, the majority of the time, losses like this are based on the sales rep's approach with the prospect.

Try to think back to a significant purchase you made. Perhaps you bought a new car. I will bet that you liked the person who sold you the car. You probably looked at similar cars in other dealerships, but when you finally met this particular salesperson, you bought from them. Why? Because you trusted them. You liked them, and you felt comfortable throughout the experience.

This is important to understand because products and services are essentially interchangeable, but a prospect's sales experience is key. A big part of a prospect's sales experience involves the sales rep's approach. Yes, there are circumstances where a prospect needs a specific item and must buy it regardless of who is involved. When a purchase is made from necessity, a sales rep's approach is inconsequential.

However, when a prospect has time to make a decision, they will put a lot of emphasis on how the rep made them feel.

The same concept rings true in a sales job application process. Sales managers weigh a candidate's approach much higher than other factors. They are about to make a significant investment in you as a candidate, and they will subconsciously put emphasis on how you made them feel throughout the process. If you are at 200% of your quota but act like a jerk, your performance is irrelevant. With a high volume of candidates on the market today, most appear to be interchangeable. Even if your Resume and LinkedIn are on par with Mark Cuban, you must still be aware of your approach with sales managers. The smallest detail can separate you from the pack. If you are unaware of how you are being perceived, you might not understand that your approach is holding you back, and you'll waste time wondering what's wrong.

Years ago, I interviewed a rep in Vancouver who was at 0% of quota. HR cautioned against his poor attainment, but I loved the approach he took with me in setting up an initial meeting. It demonstrated to me that if he were hired, he would be able to get in touch with our prospects very easily. I take care of teaching him to follow our particular sales process. He would be a strong addition to the team.

At the same time, I was interviewing another rep who finished at 194% of quota. His approach during the entire process was terrible. He barely looked me in the eyes, never smiled, and mumbled when he talked. I didn't feel comfortable around him, and I would not feel comfortable putting him in front of our prospects. Yet HR was encouraging me to hire him based on his numbers.

Here I am with one candidate at 0% and the other at 194%. One was tremendous when it came to how he approached the sales job application process, and the other didn't even understand how to interact professionally. I enthusiastically vouched for the 0% candidate with HR and stressed that a sales candidate's approach should be weighted more heavily in this type of evaluation.

I was successful in getting the 0% rep in the door. In his first year, he led my team and overachieved on quota. I saw on LinkedIn that the other rep bounced around a few other companies. He had great numbers, but it was how I felt during my experience with him that made it an easy decision.

Sales managers think of candidates from the perspective of their prospects. How you make a sales manager feel will be how you make a prospect feel. This is why your approach is weighted heavier in a sales job application process than in other types of job application processes.

If you were applying to be an accountant, no one would care how you went about setting up the interview because it is not part of the criteria of what makes a good accountant. In sales, the method and behaviors you demonstrate in pursuit of your interview are direct indicators of how you'll perform in the role.

It is more common to proceed in a sales job application process with a below-average resume than with a below-average approach. The same is true in the sales cycle. Going back to that Microsoft example... If you have an inferior product, but you provide the prospect with a great buying experience, you can win. Whereas if you have the best product and provide a haphazard experience for the buyer, you will most likely lose.

I will show you how to have such a solid approach to this process that sales managers everywhere will start to vouch for you as their next hire, regardless of your experience or past performance. Now that you understand the importance let's get back to who you should be targeting.

Target List

This part is going to be much more exciting than preparing your Resume and updating your LinkedIn. Go grab a coffee and a pen. Set aside some time for yourself, throw on Spotify, and get comfortable. This is the fun part of my process, but it still works. It's time to make a list of target companies. Start by writing down any company in the world where you'd like to work someday.

"What if I don't know any companies where I might want to work?" If you can't think of something specific, then start by thinking big picture. Think about the companies you buy from, companies you've seen on TV, or ones you've heard about online. Maybe it's Sephora? Google? That start-up your friend told you about? Tesla? A yacht brokerage? Wal-Mart?

This is a brainstorming exercise that kickstarts my Targeted Networking section. It is designed to mirror the part of a real sales process referred to as prospecting. Before you can begin prospecting, your sales manager must provide you with a list of target companies. The big difference between a real sales process and my sales job application process is that you are not given a list from anyone. It is entirely up to you to pick your target list.

Your target list does not have to be limited to companies that you randomly brainstorm. You can do a little bit of research if you like. When I decided to get into sales, it took a while. I kept changing my list of companies until I realized that I wanted to target ones that paid the highest commission. I Googled "companies that pay the highest commission."

Sit back, drink your coffee, listen to some music, and make your target list. This first group of companies is going to be referred to as your A-List. It is important not to get too bogged down on the details. Your A-List is made up of the companies you would give an arm and a leg to if they offered you a sales job.

Okay, great. Your A-List is done. It is time to make your B-List. In terms of brands or household names, your B-List may look a little less glamorous than your A-List. It is going to be made up of those companies that already have people from your current network in them.

Think of your neighbors, college alumni, your cousin, that person you met at a cafe, or your colleagues from previous jobs. Start brainstorming where your network is employed and start writing these companies down. If your brother-in-law is always talking about how his sister works at Workday, write down her name, and write down Workday.

Your B-list will be a little longer than your A-List. It may even seem like you are extending too deep out into your network, but that is okay. We are just making a list. I am not asking you to randomly call up your brother-in-law's sister and ask her if Workday is hiring. We aren't there yet. We are just writing out your B-list.

If there is an overlap between your A-List and B-List, that is a good thing. Having a company on both lists means that you have a desire to work there, and you also know one of their employees. Another way to build out your B-List is to look through your LinkedIn contacts and start scanning for people in sales that you believe are doing well. If you are thinking, "There is no way that Jimmy from freshman year is going to want to help me get a job at Microsoft." Those are totally normal thoughts. However, trust me on this and write down Jimmy from freshman year – Microsoft.

We will work on how to make your approach with Jimmy's work later. Don't worry. People in sales absolutely love talking to other people about their success. Jimmy would love to tell you how awesome Microsoft is and why he is doing so well there. Once you feel good about your B-List, you're done with it. You don't have to put companies on your list just to increase the number of targets. Remember, every company you add at this point is up to you.

Most candidates do not want to make a C-List. This is especially true for seasoned sales reps who rely heavily on their networks. They usually assume that they will get a job at one of their A-List targets, and if not, they'll at least get a job one on their B-List. This is not the best practice.

You should develop a C-list for two reasons. First, building out a C-list allows you to go out and practice my process in real life. It is a huge advantage to talk with gatekeepers and sales managers at companies on your C-list before you have that big, intimidating sales interview at an A-List company.

The same idea is true in sales. If you have a few sales calls with prospects who are lower on your target list, you are going to be well prepared when you finally get a shot at your top targets. By no means do you have to practice with a C-List account before moving to a B-List account. I am simply suggesting that the more times you can run through my process, the better grasp you will have on how it works. You can never underestimate the benefits of repetitions.

The second reason for having a C-List is that you may actually like one of these companies better than ones on the other list. When I applied to college, I did attend the best school I got into. I ended up going to a college where I felt most comfortable on campus. You might have a similar experience with a company on your C-List.

Your C-List might be smaller companies that you come across that seem interesting to you. You might find some on websites or forums that discuss start-ups, or if you are "old-school," you might find some through word of mouth. Word of mouth is a great way to find companies with a good solid sales culture.

Plenty of sales reps have a better quality of life selling for mid-market and start-up companies versus Google or Microsoft. By establishing an A, B, and C-list, you'll be able to sort through a wide range of sales organizations and find out which one is the best fit for you.

Next, do a bit of research on each company before even thinking about making contact. This is critical. We already went over this in Messaging Etiquette, but this is a reminder that it is important not to get too excited and shoot off an impulsive message.

Remember, no one wants their friends randomly asking them about their company, especially if you don't talk to that friend as often. No one wants to be bombarded by job seekers every time they're looking for a new job.

Start by looking at your A, B, and C-Lists and searching for sales job openings on the company websites. You will be able to consolidate some of your lists by eliminating companies that are not hiring right now. That may not eliminate those companies entirely from your list, but companies that have openings will take priority over companies that do not. This is directly related to the sales process. You have established a target list, and now you are working to prioritize and qualify companies based on more intel.

Next, you are going to take your list and open LinkedIn. LinkedIn is not only the prospecting tool for all salespeople, but it also will be your Targeted Networking tool throughout my process. Use the search bar on LinkedIn to try and locate Sales Reps, Recruiters, and Human Resources contacts at the companies on your now-prioritized list. Work your way through it from top to bottom.

When you come across these contacts, keep track of their names. I recommend setting up a spreadsheet with columns like Company, Network, Sales Rep, Recruiter, HR across the top. You can then fill the cells with the prioritized company list, who you know already from your network, and then who you find in Sales, Recruiting, and HR. If you need additional training, I have lots of additional resources at HowToGetASalesJob.com

Do not blindly reach out to any of these contacts yet. These are your second-class targets. Your first-class targets are going to be your network, and we'll get to that. However, it is important to have both lists of contacts written down or to at least make a note of who's who. If you do not find any Sales Reps, Recruiters, or HR contacts at a company, leave the fields blank.

After you are done, read the job descriptions you've found and check to see if there are any outliers that would bar you from applying. For example, watch out for things like "German-speaking is a must." You will waste precious time if you do not read postings. They may be looking for candidates who live on Mars while you live in Chicago. If you never read the description, you will waste time wondering why they aren't responding.

You don't have to get too caught up on it, but please, just use common sense. If there is a serious requirement that you cannot or do not meet, it is best to re-prioritize your list and move on. I hire in Montreal, and if a candidate does not speak French, it is a waste of time for them and for me when they reach out unknowingly.

In sales, by operating without a target list, your default strategy will be calling, emailing, texting, and reaching out to random people at random companies. Below average sales reps rely on this type of method. If you approach your sales job application process like this, it will waste a lot of your time, and you will appear to most people you encounter as someone who is aimlessly seeking any job. At all times throughout my process, you want to appear as a strategic, structured, and professional sales rep.

The Four C's of Contacting

In every other type of job application process, the part where you must contact people at one of your targeted companies tends to be very official and somewhat regulated. It typically consists of filling out an application, receiving a positive or negative response, followed by some waiting on your end.

A sales job application process provides candidates with an open opportunity to actively prospect into their targeted companies. This opportunity provides candidates with a unique ability to showcase their sales process and approach during initial interactions. Sales managers are then able to qualify candidates based on the way they approach and handle the entire application process.

A lot of candidates will initially shy away from my process when it comes to contact methods because they think it will be too aggressive. However, that is the goal. Your method of contacting targets will not only be judged by gatekeepers and sales managers, but it will also be praised by them if done properly. It is funny how many candidates tell me they would rather wait by the phone versus cold calling a sales manager. These same candidates then go on to tell me that they will explain how good they are at cold calling once they're invited in for an interview. Actions speak much louder than words. When I point out to candidates that they can use my process to demonstrate their cold calling abilities through action rather than words, most of them have an "A-ha!" moment.

If you approach things passively by filling out an application and wait for an answer, you are demonstrating that this will be the approach you use when prospecting into accounts in your territory. This will turn away a good sales manager who is looking for proactive sales reps. They want hungry, motivated reps, and they want to see you in action during the application process. At its core, sales is about the pursuit of new prospects. If you can demonstrate that you are a proactive hustler during the application process, you are demonstrating that you have the core skill needed for any open sales job.

There are four methods that can be used when it comes to contacting your target companies. I sometimes refer to them as the 4 C's of Contacting:

- Company Websites & Search Engines
- Cover Letters
- Colleagues
- Champion or Referral

Company Websites & Search Engines

This method is the one that most unfamiliar candidates will try first when looking for a sales job. This is also the method that most below-average sales reps use. Candidates who are unfamiliar with a sales job application process have never been told that it is much different from a regular job application process. For the below-average sales reps, the use of this method, there's no excuse. They should know by now that it is not a "sit and wait" process, but they're so accustomed to reacting versus pro-acting that they still default to this method of contact.

These types of candidates will go to a company's website and type in "sales job" or maybe something like, "Sales Representative at Apple." This will lead them to a generic career page with a list of open sales jobs. Once they are here, they'll click the first job that looks interesting and fill out an application with detailed information. They finish by adding references, attaching their resume, and clicking submit. Online applications take up a decent amount of time for a candidate. Once they click submit, they are done. In their mind, they have just successfully applied to Apple to become the next Sales Rep.

This is a terrible way to approach a sales job application process. It is also a good indicator that you are probably not cut out for sales. If we were to compare this to how you might go about setting up an actual sales meeting with Apple, this would be like you going to the Vendor Inquiry page on www.Apple.com and filling out a form. Your information sits in Apple's on-line filing cabinet that they check maybe once every two years. Apple would never decide to make a purchase by scanning all their Vendor Inquiries. They get millions of inquiries! In fact, I would guess that Apple has a Vendor Inquiry page set up simply to weed out vendors.

If you wouldn't do this when trying to sell something to Apple, why would you do this when trying to sell yourself to Apple?

Candidates do this because no one has told them what they should be doing instead.

Some may do it because it is comfortable, and it seems appropriate. Yes, I agree. It is also polite and easy. You can complete applications for ten companies per day and never have to interact with a single person. This is why it is such a popular method among below average and unfamiliar candidates.

What really happens when they click submit is that all their information goes into the candidate database, and then the sales manager receives an automatically generated email that states, "Susan Smith applied for the position of Sales Representative." Most sales managers will see the automatic email pop up, ignore it, and move on to more important things in their calendar.

Why do sales managers ignore system-generated emails with new candidate applications? They are looking for proactive candidates, not ones who sit at home filling out applications. When I saw these emails as a manager, my initial thought would be, "Okay, great, Susan Smith just applied. If she's good, I'm sure I'll hear from her soon."

All day long, sales managers must host forecast calls, one-on-ones, customer calls, management meetings, team meetings, and pipeline reviews. Most managers also have prior experience speaking with candidates who use this approach and find these types of candidates to be shy and introverted people, usually not cut out for sales.

This approach does not demonstrate that you are proactive and hungry in your pursuit. Remember, it is one thing to be able to tell someone that you are a good sales rep, but it is another thing altogether to be able to demonstrate this throughout the process.

Eventually, you will have to apply on-line and maybe even be asked to formally complete an application by HR later in the process. It will eventually need to happen, but Company websites and Search Engines should never be the method you attempt when it comes to contacting a target. This method provides the highest chances that you will never receive a call back regarding your candidacy. It is the most common and the least successful.

Cover Letter

In addition to system-generated emails from on-line applications, sales managers also receive several well-crafted emails directly from candidates. This is usually how most seasoned sales reps approach the application process. These emails always contain a resume, a healthy paragraph outlining their qualifications, followed by an ask for a meeting. This is referred to as a 'cover letter,' and many experts will support this method. However, I find this method to be weak at best.

When I was a manager, I would receive cover letters like this on a daily basis after posting an open job on our website. At first glance, you'd think that this appears better and more professional than an auto-email from the system, right? It is certainly a little better, but here's what happens next.

I would open a candidate's email, read it, look at the resume, and wait for a follow-up. Anyone can cut, paste, attach, and click send. By waiting, I would be able to see if the candidate demonstrates perseverance in their follow-up. What happens most of the time? No one ever follows up. Most candidates send a nice cover letter, and then they wait forever for a response.

Most candidates wait because they think that they must be respectful of a sales manager's time. Don't get me wrong; waiting is often the best practice when you are applying to other types of jobs outside of sales. Managers in other professions might be turned off by your aggressive pursuit. However, a cover letter alone in sales is a very inactive way of pursuing a job at one of your target companies. If you send an email with your resume attached and wait, you have a slightly better chance than clicking "apply" on the website, but your chances are still very low.

Some candidates will argue that they start by sending a cold email and follow it up with multiple phone calls and emails over the course of a couple of weeks. If this is done properly in a polite and professional manner, it could work out in your favor. Done incorrectly, this borders on making you seem like a crazy ex-boyfriend. I have been in the position many times where I get an email and instantly start to receive phone calls, voicemails, and emails every day after that. The messages start to get more and more desperate. Sometimes they even become passive-aggressive, intimidating, and occasionally confrontational.

Usually, I respond to a candidate's first follow-up email in a timely manner, but sometimes I am so busy managing the business that I do not see their email for a day or two. By then, I already have four or five emails from this candidate, who I have never met. The third, fourth, and fifth emails start to pick up a condescending tone. It is always something to the effect of, "I guess you are not interested in me. What's the hesitation with meeting me?" It may not be that blunt, but most managers can sense a condescending tone over email.

This hard-pressed follow-up may work for some reps when it comes to pushing for a deal at the end of a quarter. Or it may work in a tight situation where you need a response from a prospect immediately, but it is best to avoid this type of approach during a sales job application process. Never send condescending "where are you" emails to a sales manager that you have never met before. Trust me on this one. There is a right and wrong way to approach a follow-up to your cover letter. Sounding like a debt collector never works.

I did hire a candidate who followed up with me multiple times, but she did it in a very professional and respectful way. It took her almost three weeks to get time on my calendar, and by then, I appreciated her approach, and we connected very well. She never sent a phishing, "where are you" email to me, but she was indeed persistent. Every three to four days, she would send a brief follow-up email letting me know that she was still interested in the job and that she understood I might be busy. Her emails always remained short and polite, with a positive spin on the fact that she was waiting patiently for my calendar to open. This candidate also continued to provide me with open dates on her calendar.

After about the second week, I was able to respond and select a date the following week to speak with her. It was her positive and professional persistence that interested me enough to put the time in my calendar. It is difficult to do this type of follow-up to cold emails effectively, and there is a fine line that you must not cross. If you are not able to be patient, positive, and professional in your follow-ups, I do not recommend a cover letter as your preferred method of contact. You could become emotional or seem desperate, and then you are burned.

Even sales candidates with the greatest resume and most well-written cover letters can become way too persistent with following up that they disqualify themselves in the process. I caution against using this method altogether. It is too difficult to pull off. My process is all about giving you the best practice so that you have the best chance of advancing. Let's look at the final two methods to understand what's most effective.

Colleague (Connect with A Sales Rep, Recruiter, or HR)

I am introducing you to the various contact methods from the worst to best. To recap, a company website or search engine is the worst method. A cover letter is decent but only if you have a positive and professional follow-up, which is difficult to master. The third method is similar to a cover letter but more indirect in the approach. This method involves contacting a colleague, whether it be a sales rep, a recruiter, or a person in HR at one of your target companies. It avoids direct contact with the sales manager. Let's look at how to best utilize this method.

As previously discussed, a sales manager will have a flooded inbox with auto-emails from the system and cold emails from candidates. While this is happening, the sales manager will naturally start a proactive search for a candidate. The way that most sales managers start searching is by letting their immediate colleagues know about a new open headcount on their team.

When a sales rep quits, the sales manager starts by informing the current reps on his team as well as HR and the company's recruiter. The goal of letting each group know about the departure is to spread out the effort of finding the next best rep to join the team. When these colleagues hear of the opening, they'll almost always have an initial reaction.

Imagine if one of the sales rep's reaction was to turn to the manager and say, "Hey, I've actually been talking to a candidate who's looking to join our company. She has a decent resume. Do you want to talk to her?" You could be the one they're talking about!

Imagine if the recruiter got an email about the opening and replied with, "I actually know a local candidate that has been talking with me for a while now, and she is very interested." Or what if HR said, "There's a candidate who has been in our system and continues to reach out on a regular basis. I like her. Do you want me to put you in touch?"

All three of these scenarios could be you. This is what you want to happen! Why? Because if you are the candidate that these people openly offer up to the sales manager, you've just jumped ahead of all those candidates who are sitting in the manager's inbox. Remember the system-generated emails and cold cover letters? Forget about them. The sales manager will now be receiving a warm intro to you directly from a colleague. Your odds of receiving a callback will increase tremendously if this is the case.

How do you make this happen? How can you ensure you are at the front of mind with the manager's colleagues? You need to apply a type of mini-cover letter approach with each person at your targeted company on a regular basis.

While such an approach with the manager may be considered too persistent, when it is used with the surrounding colleagues, it creates a buffer. This buffer is important because it prevents you from being viewed in an aggressive manner, and it also allows you to meet the manager more organically.

You are essentially building a network of peers that the sales manager regularly discusses open positions with. This is why I refer to this part of my process as Targeted Networking. By networking within your target companies, you are breaking down a barrier of entry and positioning yourself as the next best candidate.

Remember that spreadsheet that we had you build? It should have a prioritized A, B, and C-List of companies with names of sales reps, recruiters, and HR people. It also has a list of people in your current network. We'll get to your network more when using contact method number four, champion, or referral, but for now, we'll use the spreadsheet to guide us in our outreach.

Feel free to start with a quick refresher on our messaging etiquette from before if you need it. Once you feel comfortable, we're going to use email and LinkedIn messaging to contact the sales manager's colleagues directly. The object of any email or LinkedIn message is to describe a scenario or situation briefly and then make a professional request to secure the next step.

Use the following as a framework and tailor your message to suit individual sales reps, recruiters, and HR contacts. For more information visit HowToGetASalesJob.com

Hi, Recruiter,

My name is John Davis, and I am currently an intern at Samsung. I am actively searching for sales rep positions and wanted to introduce myself and ask if we could discuss the opening at Apple in Denver for the position of Junior Sales Representative. I usually have mornings open before 9 am or am free in the evenings after 4:30 pm.

Please let me know if you are open to having a call, and I can coordinate.

Best,
John

Hi HR Analyst,

My name is John Davis, and I am currently an intern at Samsung. I came across the position of Junior Sales Representative on your site and wanted to reach out in order to determine the most appropriate way to proceed in the application process. Would it be possible to have a conversation with you or potentially the recruiter or sales manager in charge of hiring for this position? I am available on Thursday afternoon or Friday morning next week. Please let me know if we can chat, as I'd love to learn more.

Best,
John

Hi, Sales Rep,

I am looking at an open Sales position at Apple and wanted to reach out to see if you had some time to discuss your experience and career to date. I know you are busy, so I wouldn't ask for much time, but if you had thirty minutes later next week, I would really appreciate your perspective and time. Either way, I hope to hear from you.

Best,
John

Each message should have a different flavor. The sales rep email is the most informal and least structured. The HR email references understanding the hiring process. The recruiter email asks to specifically and formally discuss the position. The point here is to open a line of communication with each person and request the next step. Regardless of each person's response, you'll want to be sure you adhere to all the phone and messaging etiquette that I have provided earlier. At this point, it is important to respect their time if they are kind enough to give it to you.

You may even send a similar message to someone in your extended network when using this method. By no means are you limited to just these positions at a target company. If you want to pursue other employees who you think you might have a chance with, that is also an effective method.

I advise against blasting messages out to every person at the company, especially if it is a smaller company. You never want to appear desperate or unprofessional when using this method. Successful sales reps would never blast messages to every person at one of their prospects. The same rules apply.

If you have trouble at any point identifying an open role or other details about an opening, try to generalize your messaging. It's better to approach with a general message of interest than to wait around for exact details. Do not worry if all the details are not available. I still encourage you to begin messaging these people regardless.

Secure an Interview

The goal of any interaction that you have with these people is to network, so they remember you and then move the ball forward toward securing a phone interview with the sales manager. You are not going to get much time with each person, so it is critical that you use that time wisely. So, what should you do if they reply?

When someone responds to you, the door is open. You need to build some rapport with them quickly and let them know your story. We worked on your story already. Your story highlights your career to date and brings someone up to speed on what it is that you are looking to do next. You can inform someone within a matter of thirty seconds to a minute (or half a paragraph if via email). Your story is your elevator pitch on yourself. Don't spend all day telling it. Aren't you glad you are following my process from the ground up? See how it's building?

Once you provide your story to each person who replies to you, it is then up to you to use your interactions as a way of doing some research into the company and any open sales positions. I cannot cover every scenario that will play out, but what I will tell you is that some people will be super helpful, others will be shy, and others may be restrained and resist giving you any information. All of this is fine because this is truly just an exercise in intelligence gathering and networking at this point.

If you can be memorable while gathering information, that is optimal.

Make some notes after each interaction to understand the pulse of the organization's hiring process. If you find, after speaking to all three types of people at Apple, that the sales process is highly selective and may not be open for a few more months, that is fine. Just go back to your A, B, and C-List spreadsheet and re-prioritize. If you suddenly find that a sales rep at Google will walk your resume down the hall and hand it to the sales manager in person, that is amazing. You've just moved the ball forward at one of your targets. If done correctly, you will start to see the ball move forward at several targets. It's okay to use this approach repeatedly throughout your list, just as a sales rep would work their target account list.

This contact method is much more efficient than an online application or a cover letter. It is essentially the same technique used by reps who are prospecting into an account. They will reach out to several people in the account until they find someone to give them a warm introduction to the decision-maker. They do this versus coldly reaching out to the decision-maker because it has proven to yield higher results.

You will do this repeatedly at your target companies until you connect with similar people who will eventually guide you through the hiring process for sales reps at their company. Don't be overly aggressive. Remain polite, professional, and respectful at all times. If you are efficient enough for them to remember your approach, you will do well.

After you speak to each person, be sure to act on any advice they give you. For instance, if they tell you to email your resume directly to Joe Murphy with them in copy, you have to do it. I can't tell you how many candidates do not listen to the recommendations they get from employees at their target companies. This is a huge miss. Take their lead and follow their advice. For starters, they know how the organization operates better than you, and secondly, it reflects on your approach if you don't follow through on things.

Each time you are done interacting with a person at one of your targets, be sure to send a brief one-line thank-you note to each person. This is a must. I will cover thank-you notes in-depth later but for now, write them an email or LinkedIn message that thanks them for the time and advice. Keep it to one sentence, if possible. This is non-negotiable. I don't care how inconsequential you think your interaction was. By thanking them, you've just increased your exchanges with them and have become slightly more memorable. Perhaps they'll remember you when their sales manager lets them know of an opening.

If one of the people you contact directly introduces you to the sales manager -congratulations! If they do not introduce you but were open to speaking with you, you're still in a good position. You're building your network within one of your targets. It is okay to continue to target and contact others in the organization using this same method. The method scales very well and can be repeated within a company.

This contact method is the #1 approach that I encourage candidates to use during my process. It is the one that holds the highest yield in terms of positive responses and builds up your brand and your candidacy at each company. If you are not comfortable with this method at the start, I recommend beginning with your C-List accounts until you get better at it. Then, you can move on up to those big, bad, dream accounts on your A-List. By then, you will be a pro at this method. A lot of good things will happen when you use this method regardless of if you have to send a single message or twenty.

The goal of this contact method is not to become best friends with the people you are contacting. The goal is to learn more about the sales rep hiring process and make your presence known as a potential candidate. This knowledge will benefit you later when you do get in touch with the manager. If you do happen to succeed in getting a phone interview set up by using this method, do not get on that call until you've read my phone interview section. Remember that doing steps out of order generates less than desirable results.

If you do not get an introduction to the sales manager through one of their colleagues, do not panic. Try to build rapport with these people until it occurs organically. If time progresses and you feel comfortable asking for an introduction, that is appropriate. I suggest against asking immediately after connecting with a colleague. However, over time it may be in your best interest to ask away. Use proper judgment.

Champion or Referral

Regardless of where you are in your sales career, the absolute best contact method to use is a referral. To this day, the best sales reps I know always rely on referrals when looking for a new job. Referrals also work very well for college students trying to get their first sales job, and for other professionals who are trying to switch industries. It even works internally when reps are trying to switch teams or change locations within their current organization. There is nothing cold or warm about a referral. **A referral is the hottest and purest way of contacting a sales manager.**

A referral can also be considered your champion within a target company. In sales, we define the person at an account who is helping the rep push their product as a 'champion.' A champion is someone who wants the rep to succeed because they see the benefits. A referral should also want you to succeed in getting a job at their company because they, too, see the benefits you bring. A referral is when your friend, colleague, neighbor, cousin, etc. walks into a sales manager's office and hands them your resume. It is a direct handoff delivered with a smile, endorsement, and an established sense of trust. When someone I know hands me a resume, I will stop what I'm doing and email that candidate to set up a time to talk. Finding top-notch sales talent can be difficult, but when someone I trust makes a recommendation, I take it very seriously.

This is true for all sales managers. When they have an opening for a sales rep, they will start by taking referrals. If that fizzles out, they move on to talking to their colleagues, as we mentioned. If that fizzles out, they'll scan their inbox for cover letters. If all else fails, they'll comb through the online application system. If you noticed, this is the reverse flow of the contact methods I have provided you with. I introduced them this way so you could gradually see the increasing inefficiency. With a referral, you are putting yourself in the best possible situation of landing a phone interview.

If you are new to sales, having a network you can rely on is everything. It is important to start slowly and continually work on building up your network. A great way to build your network out is by offering help to those in need without asking for anything in return. Favors. Favors are a great way to build your network. Over time, you will find that a lot of your network is willing to return the favor when you are in need.

If you believe you already have a strong network, you will need to assess how people in your network view you. Are you someone who helps others? Are you trustworthy? Is the relationship one-sided? It's important to know where you stand with others.

In short, if you are going to actively reach out to people and ask that they vouch for you, you must be willing to do the same thing. If you are working as a sales rep for Boeing and someone in your network reaches out to discuss sales positions at Boeing, you should be open to having this type of conversation. The more doors you help open, the more your network will grow. Imagine you never respond to this person's request, and they go on to become the EVP of Sales at Walmart someday… You missed out on a huge opportunity to better your network.

It is not necessary to walk down the hall to your boss's office every time someone contacts you to talk about working at Boeing. However, when you have an honest and open conversation with someone about potentially interviewing at Boeing, it is a good gesture to provide guidance on how to approach them. Always remember to use your best judgment with others before recommending them to your manager. If you become the sales rep who just asks everyone for favors and never gives any in return, you will quickly be labeled as selfish, and you will find the referral game actually working against you.

You never want to become known as a selfish person in sales. If others perceive you this way, and you ask for them for a referral, they could easily walk into their manager's office and say, "Hey, John Davis is going to apply here. Don't hire him. He's selfish." Boom. You are dead in the water.

You must understand the sensitivity around using your network in sales. The main lesson here is that networks work both ways. If you are genuine and respectful, I assure you that you will find yourself being referred to more open sales positions despite your credentials. If you are a jerk, you will probably find getting a referral very difficult. Be a good person and build your network naturally over time by helping other people out. It will help you get referred to more open sales positions.

Lastly, to land a referral, just use common sense in your approach. A situation could come up at a party, over coffee, or maybe through a text. At some point, you are going to have to explain your story to someone, express your interest in working in sales at his or her company, and inquire about the sales manager or hiring process. It may sound strange when I say to use common sense. However, if you are asking for a referral from your network, I assume that you must have an established relationship with the person. You should not be asking for a referral from people you don't know already know well.

After you ask your friend, things will fall into place naturally, and you will find that (if you are a good person), they will lead you in the right direction. It is important to follow through on the action items that they give you so you can continue moving in the direction they're leading you. If you fail to follow through, they will think that you weren't too serious, and they will move on to do other more important things. Even worse, if that happens and then you ask for a referral from them later in life, they'll remember you never followed through before, and they will be less likely to help you.

Be respectful of those in your network. Follow through and follow up on action items that they tell you about when they are going to make a referral on your behalf. It puts you in a good spot with them and with the sales manager they are referring you to. This will go a long way in getting in contact quicker with more sales managers and naturally building your network up over time.

Follow Up

In sales, if you do not follow up with people, they will notice. Once they notice, they will start to expect less from you. This is not good when it comes to your peers or management, but imagine if your prospects start to expect less from you? If this happens, you are going to make fewer connections at your target accounts and bring in less revenue.

Why am I only discussing follow-up now? Well, you have just begun contacting, interacting, and corresponding with all kinds of different people at your target companies, and now they are starting to respond to you. When they respond, they will most likely ask you for action. This means that it is your turn to take some action and follow up with them to ensure it is taken care of. Let's look at an example.

If a recruiter responds to you via email with something like, "I'm not seeing the job code you provided in your email. Can you please send it to me again?" You must be sure that you send it to her again. If your sister-in-law at Workday asks you, "Can you please reach out to Sara.Jones@yahoo.com and copy me? Sara is great, and she can help you out."

You must email Sara Jones and copy your sister-in-law. Some people may think that this is all common sense, but I can't stress enough how important this is. **It may be a "friendly ask" to**

people in real life, but to people in sales, this is referred to as a follow-up. It is taking proactive action on the conversation at hand. It is important to do this. If you are unsure of the person's request or action they want you to take, it is on you to clarify.

For instance, your sister-in-law asks you, "Can you please reach out to Sara Jones about this and copy me?" You must reply with, "Yes, of course. What is her email address?" It is perfectly acceptable to clarify something before you follow up or act. It shows that you are aware and capable. When you are unsure what someone means, be professional and direct. Do not send an even more confusing email back. Just clarify what you do not understand and make your next move.

Once you are committed to following up on actions given to you from your network, a sales rep, recruiter, HR, or anyone else at your target companies, you will find yourself moving through the contact part of my process at a steady pace. These people will provide you with actions that will lead you towards connecting with someone else at the company. That next person is just as important to contact and follow up with as they may be the final step before receiving an invitation for a phone interview with the sales manager.

Most likely, you will have to repeat this part of the process a couple of times over. For instance, let's say your sister-in-law asks you to reach out to Mary Margaret at Workday. Mary Margaret asks that you reach out to Travis Williams. Travis may ask you to contact Heather LaGamba. Perhaps Heather is the sales manager, or perhaps not. **You must be patient and**

systematic in your approach and never overwhelm people that are helping you. With every interaction, you must act on the follow-ups and continue to move forward. If you find yourself stuck at any point in the process, take a deep breath, and evaluate your contact method, approach, and follow-up.

Are you describing the situation at hand and asking for the next steps, or are you just sending careless messages? Are you taking action on items from the people you spoke with, or are you just "sitting tight"? Sales is a proactive process, and so is my sales job application process. It is your job to constantly move the ball forward, and following up is a key measurement of action

Let's pretend that you've been through several iterations at a target company. Finally, one of the recruiters you messaged at Yahoo reaches out to let you know that the sales manager is named Sara Jones, and she's the one you need to contact directly about the open position. Yahoo is on your A-List, and you are extremely excited to find out Sara is the correct person to contact. What do you do? How do you follow up on this information?

You will approach Sara Jones with the same messaging that you used with every other person throughout my process. You will write a professional and polite email that includes what has happened to date (describing the situation) and then ask her for the next step. It must be brief, professional, and direct. Because you have been interacting with multiple people at the company already, your email will have more impact than a cold email would.

Your email to Sara should look something like this:

> Hi, Sara,
>
> We have not met yet, but my name is John Davis. I have been referred to you by your recruiter, Tim Thran, in hopes of setting up a conversation about the open Sales Rep role on your team. I have included my resume for your reference and am available at the following times next week.
>
> > Monday, 9 am – 2 pm
> > Tuesday, 3 pm onward
> > Thursday, 10 am – 3 pm
>
> Please let me know if you are available for a call during any of these times, and I will send an invitation.
>
> Best Regards,
>
> John

What you'll notice here is that this is very similar to most of the other emails you have sent so far in my process. Just because you've finally found the correct person in Sara Jones does not mean that you must change up your entire approach. I've had candidates who argue that because Sara is in charge, she needs to know that they were Captain of a D1 Field Hockey team in college or how they "really clicked" with the recruiter last week. None of this is important.

What is important is that you describe the situation at hand and ask Sara for the next steps. That is what a good sales rep would do during a sales process, and that is all that you should do. By doing this, you have left the ball in her court. You have asked for the next step, and you are done...for now.

Sara is going to reach out with a time to talk. When she does this, you need to thank Tim Thran and any others who have helped you secure the meeting with Sara. You do not need to send these people a detailed email, but you do need to let them know that you are going to talk to Sara soon, and you are thankful for their help along the way.

Why thank these people and provide them with an update on where you are in the process? Well, they may be your future coworkers. They also may talk to Sara at lunch or in a meeting, and when they do, they will know that you have reached out to her. This way, if your name comes up, both Sara and these people will be talking about you, which is a good thing.

If Sara does not reach out for a time to talk, you should plan to follow up on your email once a week. At the same time, you can reach out to Tim each week and let him know that you have emailed Sara and have not heard back. To signal a clear action, it is best if you ask Tim if he can chat about what comes next, or if you should continue to wait to hear from Sara.

This is the best practice for following up once you understand who oversees hiring for the open position. If you continue this process of follow up, Sara and Tim will eventually talk and get back to you. If you go three weeks with no answer, it is time to move on to the next target on your list. Do not change your approach or become controversial at this point. Three weeks without an answer means something has happened that is out of your control. Keep in mind that the pursuit of a call with Sara should not be your only active pursuit at this time.

If you have followed my process correctly, you have most likely been working long and hard for the past few weeks. At this point, you might have anywhere from four to five phone interviews at several of your target companies. This number depends on how often you repeat my process.

If you are taking a systematic approach and not just putting all your eggs in one basket, you might have something like three C-List interviews, two B-List interviews, and this potential A-List phone interview with Sara that you are still pursuing. This is a healthy level of activity.

You might only have this one phone interview lined up with Sara because you are taking it slow. The volume of interactions and contacts during my process is entirely up to you and your work ethic. If you want a lot of phone interviews, you'll need to put in a lot of work. If you want to pursue one company, you'll put in more targeted work and less volume. The same concept applies to a sales job in real life.

This call with Sara might have stemmed from any one of the several messages you sent to employees at Yahoo. Sometimes it is your first message, and sometimes it is your sixth. It all depends, but it is important to remember that your approach is being evaluated. More contact certainly sounds effective, but there is a delicate balance between more and too much. If you feel you are borderline too much, you probably are. Step back and re-evaluate.

In sales, you will close more revenue if you generate more initial meetings with prospects. In my process, you will set up more phone interviews if you contact more people at your target companies. If you only want to sell to one company, all your effort will be focused on that company. We use the same principle in my process. If you only want to work at one company, all your effort is focused on that company. It is best practice to diversify if you want to sell more or have more job offers, but in the end, the choice is entirely up to your desired outcome.

Just remember that too much of anything is bad for you. Be thoughtful and aware of how you approach each target, and you will see tremendous results.

It worked. Sara replied. Wait for a second; you are going to talk to Sara? What does that mean? Congratulations! You have just set up a phone interview!

John P. Davis

Chapter 7: Phone Interview

B efore an in-person interview, you will have a phone interview. Before a phone interview, you will have essentially already interviewed. What does that mean?

"You have already interviewed."

A manager of mine at Deutsche Bank used to always say this out loud whenever someone brought up an upcoming interview. He would look around, smile, and announce it to anyone on the floor. He was exactly right. Before any type of interview, the interviewer has already evaluated you.

Once your interview is scheduled, it is too late to change anything about yourself. The sales manager has most likely Googled you, read your resume, creeped your LinkedIn, and even made calls to other people to find out more about you. Regardless of whether it's a phone interview or in-person, this is the norm everywhere. Managers do this to hedge against their upcoming assessment of you during the actual interview

Sales managers research candidates prior to an interview because hiring is such a big decision that has a financial impact on them. The research allows them to prepare strategically for the upcoming interview. It is also a natural tendency to want to know more about someone before meeting them for the first time.

Prospects will do the same thing before a meeting with you about your product. There is a high probability that they have already read reviews on your website or perhaps even talked to someone who has used it. Start thinking about your upcoming phone interview the same way you'd think about a call with a prospect.

If you have not followed my process correctly so far, you may have some holes in your resume, LinkedIn, or in your overall approach. It is too late to change any of that now. If you have followed along correctly, you will not have to worry about being researched. You can focus on the phone interview. It is important to understand that before you have this call, and before you have any type of interview in the future, research has been done, and "you've already interviewed."

A phone interview is like the initial call a rep would have with a prospect, often referred to as a "discovery call." Both calls will contain a million different "what if" scenarios. There will be outliers and things you cannot control. I urge you to remain calm at all times. While I cannot script every call for you, I will provide you with a framework full of my best practices. The framework is something you can work back to whenever a call seems to be getting away from you.

I will break down my framework into easy to follow steps, but regardless of anything else, you must always be on your A-game. **It is a huge mistake when candidates take a phone interview lightly.** Would you take a prospect call lightly? No. A poor phone interview will diminish your chances of getting the job, and it could also damage your entire sales brand.

Let's say you have a terrible phone interview. Time passes, and that manager moves to another company on your target list. You will forever be known to them as the candidate who bombed the phone interview. If your name comes up at the new company, the manager will be quick to say, "No, thank you." There are downstream repercussions to your performance on these calls.

You will more than likely be speaking with your future sales manager. It is possible you will speak with another influencer within the organization. This could be an employee that the manager trusts. Regardless of who you are speaking with, a phone interview is a serious step, and you must be ready to rock.

My process teaches you to focus on the task at hand so you can move the ball forward without going down a rabbit hole.

Reminder: Please revisit my phones skills from earlier and make sure you understand proper phone etiquette before we look at my framework.

The Task

What is the task at hand? What is the goal of this phone interview?

Your only goal is to <u>confirm an in-person interview</u> with the person on the other line. Some candidates believe that it is an opportunity to close the sales manager by asking for the job. However, most companies are not even allowed to formally offer you a job before meeting you in-person. Therefore, if you go for the hard close too early, it will demonstrate that you don't know what you're doing. It is also presumptuous, and they might laugh you off, thinking you do not understand how to conduct a phone interview. Try not to get ahead of yourself.

By securing an in-person interview, you will be able to learn more about your future manager and have a better idea of the company, culture, and environment. Trying to seal a job offer over the phone is not the best practice. The same is true in sales. You should never try to sell your product on the first phone call. A rep's only goal on the initial call is to try to secure an in-person meeting.

Try not to think too much about sounding impressive or wanting to tell your entire life story. You can expand and elaborate more comfortably when you meet them in person. For now, you have one task. Everything else is insignificant.

And honestly, if someone offers you a job after a thirty-minute phone interview, you should be worried. They may be desperate for reps and are experiencing high turnover. **When you're on a phone interview, you just need to focus on trying to secure an in-person interview**. If you focus on this one task, you will have the clarity needed to ace the call.

Responding to the Sales Manager's Email

Let's continue our phone interview role-play with "Sara Jones." To refresh, you have already completed the following steps in my process:

1. Updated your Resume and LinkedIn profile

2. Researched your A, B, and C-List Targets

3. Targeted your network at companies and made contact

4. One of those gatekeepers, Tim Thran, sent your resume and contact information to Sara Jones

5. You followed up with Sara, and she wants to talk

6. You thanked Tim via email and are now in the process of setting up the phone interview with Sara

Sara emails you to ask if you are available at 3 pm, Friday, 2 pm on Tuesday, or any time on Wednesday next week. What do you do? Panic? No. Stick to my process.

Remember how we started building your resume by looking at how to write your name? That was a fundamental exercise. The first thing you must do before responding to Sara is also fundamental: check your calendar.

It may seem simple, but a lot of candidates get excited and respond right away, saying Friday will work because they want the first opening. The next day, they realize they have a mandatory work meeting on Friday from 1-3 pm. Now they must go back and forth with Sara to reschedule. This is already demonstrating that you struggle with time management. Although it may seem minor, always check your calendar.

Although it is basic, this is what you would do if a prospect asked about your availability. For some reason, when it is a sales manager, candidates throw their fundamentals out the window and just want to respond as quickly as possible. I've come to learn that it is just nerves.

It looks like you are open on Tuesday at 2 pm, so let's role-play a little bit. It is best to be formal in your response when accepting a time to speak. Formalities always trump informalities in email. If you are trying to play it cool or sound like a schmooze, it can come across as rude and pretentious. Think about when you are emailing someone, and you ask, "How are you?" If they respond, "Not bad," you immediately start to wonder, "Not bad? What's wrong?" If they had responded, "I am good, how are you?" There is no room for misunderstanding. The same applies to your email in this situation. Don't ever try to play it cool. Play it professionally.

Simple, professional, and formal.

> Hi Sara,
>
> Tuesday at 2 pm works great for me. My cell is 555-2010. I will send a calendar invitation now for our call. I look forward to speaking with you.
> Best Regards,
> John

Some experts might suggest that you begin your email by thanking Sara. I disagree with this and tend to shy away from thanking someone right off the bat. It can come off as desperate. By being overly thankful that she has agreed to a call may tip her off that you don't have many job opportunities, and you are dying to talk to her. Remember… no one wants to talk to a desperate person.

Being polite is not desperate. Being direct and letting Sara know your availability, your contact information, and outlining the next step is extremely professional. A professionally written email shows Sara that you will be ready for the meeting, as opposed to showing her just how thankful you are for the meeting.

On a separate but related note: in all your correspondence throughout my process…. Please do not use exclamation points in an email!! I mentioned this earlier, but again, do not use them. They look immature and make you seem desperate!!! Double-check your spelling and respond to Sara's email. What's next?

From an administrative perspective, it is up to you to send out the calendar invitation. The only reason not to do this is if she mentions that she will send one out. If she does not mention it, take the initiative, and let her know you will do it and then do it. If you say you are going to do something, you must make sure you do it. Actions speak louder than words, remember? If you say you are going to do something during my process and fail to do it, the other person will take it as a sign of disrespect or incompetence. They will keep looking for a candidate who acts on their word.

Let's recap a few housekeeping items. Do not respond from a strange email address. Do not send a 5-bullet agenda, and please make sure you use the proper time zone. The first two points almost always happen. You must avoid these at all costs. The strange email address is just paying attention to detail, and the 5-bullet agenda is just overkill. You are demonstrating that you will be the sales rep who will try to fit in forty-one PowerPoint slides on a thirty-minute call. Don't do it. Just schedule the call.

The time zone issue is a common mistake, but it can happen. Candidates mess up the time zone on a calendar invite, and then I get to listen to them spend the first five minutes of their precious phone interview explaining to me how they forgot I was Eastern Time. It's simple enough to know why this should matter. Get your timing right.

Calendar Invite

Try to be lean and clean with your calendar invitation. Send it out for thirty minutes at 2 pm EST Tuesday. Include the title of your meeting "Phone Call w/ John Davis" and include a location. Since it is a phone call, the location can say, "Sara, to call John at 555-2010." Include your up-to-date resume in the invite attachment as well.

Most calendar invitations have a field for location, and typically people will put a conference line if multiple people are joining the call. Your phone interview is one-on-one, so just include your cell phone number. Be sure to include the instructions because this information will be going straight into her calendar.

Stop and think about the real-world situation at hand.

Sara probably has five to ten sales reps working for her with constant back to back calls. She is busy every day. On the other hand, you are going to be sitting around, waiting for her to call you on Tuesday afternoon. It is the highlight of your week. By putting the instructions in your invitation, you will help guide her eyes on that day. If your resume is attached, you will save her from digging through her inbox to find it again. This shows Sara that you can anticipate a prospect's needs. If you do not provide clear instructions, she may miss out on calling you altogether.

Sometimes sales managers leave you hanging. Don't freak out about it or take it personally. If you are unfamiliar with sales, it is helpful to understand this may happen to you. Sales is an unpredictable job, and many managers are under pressure to deliver results. A missed phone interview could happen to you for several reasons that are out of your control. However, it is more likely to happen if you leave out instructions or make it too difficult to figure out who's calling who. If you ever find yourself sitting by the phone without an incoming call, wait 20 minutes. Don't jump the gun and react too soon—it might seem desperate, and she may call you 8 minutes later. I advise you to wait at least 20 minutes and then send a polite email like this:

> Hi, Sara,
>
> I know that we had a call on the calendar today for 2 pm, and I was hoping we could reschedule. Please let me know another day and time that work well for you this week.
>
> Best,
>
> John

This is the proper way to go about a missed call, and most sales managers will reach out to you right away once they see your email. They may feel bad and apologize because they really did get pulled into something else. It is very important not to overreact in your messaging. They will eventually respond, I promise. If they never respond to that, move on to another company; they are not worthy of your time.

The only goal of your calendar invite is to keep it clean and simple with your resume attached. My method of setting up the phone interview is direct and professional, but it is also very important to understand the reasoning behind it.

Sara has already agreed to speak with you. There is nothing else that you can do right now between her email response and your phone interview. Anything extra you do could jeopardize your chances. You must stick to my process. It allows you to demonstrate through action (not words) that you have done this before and can do it again. Clear, measurable, repeatable action shows your worth as a candidate.

Sara will be relieved at 1:45 pm when she sits at her desk and sees an informative calendar invitation from her soon-to-be new sales rep. And look! The invitation has clear instructions with a cell phone number listed, and the resume is attached. Perfect. She will subconsciously think that you have done this before, and you will be able to do it again with prospects. The phone interview has not even started, and you are already making a positive impact on Sara with your actions. This is key.

The Actual Phone Call

It's now Tuesday afternoon, and just as your phone starts ringing, you realize Nature is also calling…

It may seem obvious, but be sure to use the bathroom at 1:40 pm, if possible. Do not make the rookie mistake of waiting until 1:58 pm. For some reason, when we're mentally preparing for an important call, sometimes it slips our minds.

Once you're finished, you should spend the final 10 minutes before the call reminding yourself of your goal and how you plan to run the call. Sales reps will spend at least 10 minutes preparing their plan for a prospect's call. The same strategy applies to you in this situation. Remind yourself to focus on achieving your one goal: secure an in-person interview. With that goal in mind, we will dive into the mechanics of how you should run the call.

Greeting

Remember, Sara is calling you. You know that she is calling you. Sara knows that she is calling you. (At this point, your friends and family probably know she is calling you.) Do not make the mistake of letting your guard down and answering her call with, "Hello…?" Do not make the mistake of being too chummy and saying, "Hi, Sara!"

You want to demonstrate to Sara that you are a strong sales rep over the phone; it is critical that you stick to my process and answer your phone with the professional greeting we rehearsed.

"Hi. Good afternoon, this is John speaking."

Sara will take it from here. She is in sales and knows how to talk on the phone. I want to remind you that although your greeting is critical, it is important for you to just be human. Sara may say things like, "Hi John, it's Sara. How are you?" Tell her how you are and ask her how she is. These are common conversational phrases that people use all over the world every day, but for some reason, during a phone interview, candidates panic. It is okay to be yourself. You don't need to exaggerate anything after your greeting.

If she asks something simple like, "Does this time still work?" Try being relaxed and respond with, "Yes, this works great." Be agreeable and assure her that you are free to talk. Your greeting is structured, but after that, you are using basic communication skills - no need to be a grammatical nerd or over the top with any of this initial small talk.

Transitioning Into The Call

Sara will most likely be late for the call. Most sales managers are notoriously late for phone interviews. This is not intentional rudeness on their part. It is real life, and this is just how a sales manager's schedule typically works. Very rarely will you find someone who calls you right at 2:00 pm. Be patient and when they apologize for being late, just tell them that it is alright, and you are still available to talk. **If you do happen to point out that she's late, you will not get the job.**

It is also crucial to be aware that she may throw you a curveball after your greeting. She may tell you something like she has to put you on hold or call you back in five minutes. Or she may jump right in and ask you a few questions. For example, "So, you spoke with Natalie earlier? How'd that go?"

Another curveball might be something simple and innocent like, "Oh, you are from California? I bet the weather is amazing. It always seems to rain on Tuesdays in New York." This is small talk and very typical. All sales managers were once reps themselves, and they have engaging personalities. It is perfectly fine to chat in your spare time, but not now. Small talk like this is a trap for you.

If you buy into this small talk, you will find yourself talking about the weather in California for three minutes, followed by a trip to Napa Valley for two minutes, and maybe end with a three-minute chat about the wildfires. This puts you eight minutes into your thirty-minute call, and you haven't talked about anything. Many candidates think that this type of talk is fine, and it will help them in the long run. But I promise you that it is actually a bad thing. Sara will remember you as someone she can shoot the breeze with, but her memory will remain unclear as to how strong of a sales candidate you are.

There is no limit as to what this small talk might entail. It typically will be related to weather, traffic, or sports. If this is where you spend the bulk of your time with Sara, she will assume this is how you will spend your time on the phone with prospects.

I knew a sales manager who would engage in elongated small talk purposely with candidates. He would see how long he could get a candidate talking about random things. He would ask, "Oh yeah, it is amazing in California, but what are the winters like?" Two minutes later, he would ask, "Do you have a car, what kind?"

He claimed that a weak salesperson would keep talking about random things because they want to appear relatable. Sometimes they would talk for forty-five minutes about the Red Sox! Imagine their face after hanging up and someone asking them, "Well, how'd it go?" It is typically at this point that they realize they just talked about nonsense and never discussed the job.

If you called prospects up and just talked about the weather, you'd never sell anything. **You must be thinking about your phone interview as if it were a prospect call.**

Back to the small talk with Sara…you must remain polite and never cut Sara off directly or abruptly. If you do find her small talk persisting, the best approach is to just slow down your responses to her questions. When you are ready to stop engaging in the small talk, take a deep breath, and let out a filler word followed by a transition word.

Filler words can be things like, "Oh man…", "Yeah…", "I know…", "Right…" or many others. Transition words are things like, "Anyways…", "So…", "To start…".

The three dots after your filler word are key. You say, "Yeah…" and the three dots are a quick pause. I encourage you to use this technique to break up the conversational pattern that's about to occur. If you do not use a filler and transition word, you might be stuck saying something like, "I'd like to get back to the conversation at hand." This may come off as condescending and possibly even rude. Avoid that at all costs and use a filler plus transition. If you nail this properly, it's time to jump right into your introduction. You take control and kick off the call!

How's that for a concept? You take control of the phone interview. You will learn to love this technique after doing it effectively a few times. It is on you to kick off a prospect call, so why wouldn't you kick off a phone interview?

It may look something like this:

> *"Hi, good afternoon. This is John speaking."*
>
> *"Hi John, it's Sara. How are you?"*

"I am good, thanks. How are you?"

"I am good, too. Sorry, I am late."

"Oh, no problem."

"I see you are in California. The weather in California is so nice. You are lucky."

"I know. I love it out here. How about New York?"

"Ugh… it's like 35° today and cloudy. I was freezing on the subway ride in. We have just so many people on the subways wearing winter jackets now, so you know how that is."

"Totally… Anyways… Thank you for taking the time this afternoon."

See how that works? In fifteen to thirty seconds, you just demonstrated to your future sales manager that you can deliver a professional greeting and redirect a conversation to assume control while remaining professional along the way. This is not rude. This is how you run a sales call properly.

Agenda

It is now your turn to set an agenda for the rest of the call. If you were to call a prospect, you would also want to set an agenda with them about what you are hoping to achieve on the call. It is the same process with Sara. You must be able to sprinkle some of your own personality into the following agenda framework.

> "I wanted to talk to you today about a few things. First, I want to let you know a little bit about myself: who I am, and where I started. Then I thought we could talk about how I got to where I am today and learn a little more about the open role."

This is simple and without much personality. I want you to make it your own. There are over one hundred different versions of how you can state an upfront agenda like this, but the key here is to be brief and rehearsed. It should take you no more than fifteen to twenty seconds when saying it out loud.

When you are done saying this, you should finish with, "Does that sound okay to you?" Some people recommend saying, "Does that sound fair?" or, "Sound good to you?" Whatever comes out more naturally is fine in this situation. The key is that you are asking for Sara's validation of your agenda. The question also cites the end of your introduction and gives Sara a chance to comment on your agenda or add her thoughts on what else you may talk about.

Most sales managers will say that sounds good, and they will let you start talking. This is a double-edged sword because if you are a weak candidate, you will talk about yourself way too long and never keep the conversation moving. If Sara agrees that you can start, you must know what you are doing and how to move it forward properly. It is not an acceptance speech, and the clock is ticking... so, where do you start? Start with your story.

John P. Davis

Your Story

This is your chance to talk. You must keep your story, not one second longer than two minutes. Once, I had a phone interview with a candidate telling me his story while I sat in silence. After six minutes, I started to watch the clock. Eleven minutes later, I let out a sigh, followed by, "Wow." What did this candidate do? Oh, he kept going...

I stopped him around minute *thirteen*, and politely told him that this was not the role for him. He never knew why. It wasn't my place to tell him that he talked for thirteen minutes straight. That is a serious self-awareness flaw. It is unnatural and concerning. Regardless, six minutes would have been too long. Even three minutes pushes it into becoming borderline uncomfortable. Under two minutes should be your goal. You should be able to explain your story in under three minutes. The shorter, the better. Don't try to speak as quickly as possible... speak normally but be considerate of the clock.

If you are feeling a bit overwhelmed about your story, try to relax. This is where you will use your story that we have been using all throughout my process so far. We built, practiced, and reviewed your story earlier. We built it together from the ground up in your resume. Your resume is not only your sales tool, but it is also the outline of your story. It touches on your education, shows where you started, where you went next, how your career progressed while all along explaining sales-related activities. Your resume finishes with your current job and a two-to three- sentence objective. If you can summarize all this information in less than two minutes without going into every detail about each job, you have successfully told your story.

It is okay to begin with where you grew up and went to school, etc. as long as you don't try to tell your autobiography. I typically start with something like this, "I was born and raised in Massachusetts and went to school for Economics at Holy Cross. After that, I started my MBA at nights while working in finance for about four years."

You will notice that I left out where I went to graduate school and where I worked in finance. Remember, you are talking to a sales manager. They have glanced over your resume and realized that you are a person worth talking to. No need to sell yourself entirely just yet. You are still just summarizing an opener about yourself. Details do not matter as much as the flow of the story matters. I have covered my location, education, and the first four years of work in about seven seconds. Good pace.

Next, you will move on to your more recent experiences. It will depend on where you are in your career that will determine where you go next. Your messaging will be a little different if you are a student than if you are a long-time professional. It is best to look at a couple of examples of how this might flow.

If you are already working, your story will open like mine: covering a few talking points on your career-to-date. After that, you will naturally get more detailed in your story as you approach your current job.

If you are a student, your story will start with you explaining a bit more about the high school you went to, how you decided on your university, your field of study, and any relevant work/internships. Once you get to the internship or other jobs, then you will want to start to give a bit more detail. Work experience is usually much lighter as a student, but this is not a bad thing. It just causes you to talk more about your education before moving on to the current job or employment status.

After a quick summary of your education and work experiences (whether it be the first few jobs or something while in university), you are now at the point of your story where you will be talking about your current job. This is the most relevant information for Sara. However, you do not want to prolong this part of your story too much. Once you have introduced your current company and role, it is important to get right to it and briefly review what type of sales activities you have been performing in your current role.

Remember those sales-related activities from your resume? Remember how I harped on them and made you fill them in repeatedly? Remember the "called 40-50 people" and the "sent 10-12 emails" bullet points that we did? Now it is time to drop a couple of those in Sara's lap. Why do you want to do this? It's measurable proof of your sales skills. Here's an example of why you absolutely must talk about your sales-related activities with the sales manager.

One time, I spoke to a junior broker at a mutual fund and life insurance company. He had a solid resume, a good LinkedIn profile, and he reached out to me professionally and directly to set up a phone interview. Great start. This junior broker had a great greeting on the phone, and then he passed by some small talk and explained quickly to me that he wanted to tell me about his current role and why it is relevant to my open position. The opening was perfect.

He then went on to describe a detailed hierarchy and organizational structure within his current company. It took him a couple of minutes to explain how senior and junior brokers were compensated differently and then how the management structure worked. I found myself having to ask a few follow-up questions to clarify what he was talking about. He continued to harp on the importance of the structure of his brokerage because he was trying to account for the fact that he should actually be considered a "Senior Broker" rather than a "Junior Broker," but it was because of politics that he was stuck as a "Junior Broker."

I understood what he was talking about (internal politics can happen at companies), but it was unsettling for me. I wondered why he was telling me this and why he wasn't selling himself as my next potential sales rep.

After some time, I stopped him abruptly and asked him what he did as a "Junior Broker." This caught him off-guard. He was shocked. "What do I do? You mean like every day?" He started laughing. I repeated my question, "Yeah. What do you do every day?" He laughed again and explained that he has a book of sixty customers and calls ten to twelve each day with a structured follow-up process in order to progress his on-going sales cycles. He then went on to tell me that after he's done with his current customers, he sits down to prospect into his 2000-person contact list and makes cold calls and sends cold emails.

He found it funny that we were talking about this. He was very curious as to why I wanted to understand these things. If he had said that earlier in the interview, instead of explaining what a junior broker was, I may have hired him.

The problem was that we spent (wasted) the first ten minutes of a thirty-minute phone interview discussing his company structure and politics. Yes, I eventually redirected him to tell me about the sales-related activities that actually mattered to me, the sales manager, but I had to drag him there. I pictured him on a call with a prospect discussing company politics rather than the benefits that we could deliver. He did a great job of talking, but he did not demonstrate that he had a killer instinct for selling.

He might have been an okay sales candidate to bring in for an in-person interview, but my notes showed that he was a bit scattered in his approach to a sales call. He was more concerned with promotions and titles rather than with selling. Sales is direct. You must be direct in your phone interview and get to your sales activities quickly.

This is a lot of information to fit into a short two-minute window, so you must work on it prior to speaking with Sara. The history of your career and your sales activities is over in two minutes. To put a bowtie on your story and close it out, tell Sara your status about where you are today in your career.

Where are you today? You are interviewing with Sara Jones at Yahoo. The end should go something like this: "which brings us to today. I am looking to make my next move to Yahoo, and I think this is a great opportunity for me.

Let's remember that this is a thirty-minute phone interview. For those of you keeping track of time (which is important in sales), at this point, you should have as follows:

- 30 seconds to 1 minute for your Greeting & Small Talk

- 1-minute Agenda

- 2 minutes of your story to date

This is your goal. This is your pace, and this should be the pace of any great sales call. Do not rush to beat the clock. It is extremely important to be timely and move swiftly.

If you were to account for human nature, potential interruptions, or the fact that most sales managers are a bit late, you would find yourself right around 2:08 pm. At this point, you should be extremely excited to proceed.

My brother gave me this advice before my first ever sales interview. He is a highly successful sales rep and has been in the industry much longer than me. When I wanted to switch from finance to sales, I called him, and he gave me a mock interview over the phone.

When we were done, he said, "Dude, it sounds like you don't like finance and want to get out of it." I said, "Yeah, exactly. I hate it. I want to get into sales." He said, "Dude, no one wants to hear about you wanting to leave. They want to hear how excited you are about the potential to join their company. Hype up your excitement. You need to tell them you'd be legitimately thrilled to join them. It is obvious to anyone that you want to leave. I mean, you are actively interviewing! It's not because things are bad; it's because you are excited!"

This hit me hard. I knew this, and you probably know this too, but sometimes you just need someone else to explain why it is so important. Don't be negative about your current situation, whatever it is. It sounds pathetic, especially over the phone, talking with someone you haven't met yet. **It is important to sound excited when you finish your story.**

Tell Sara why you looked up Yahoo, why you want to work there, why you are so excited about the opportunity. Tell her it sounds awesome and say the words, "I am really excited to be speaking with you." It will work wonders. Then when you think you have got her attention, and she agrees with you a bit. You have done your job. You have told your story and conveyed excitement.........NOW PAUSE. Stop talking. Or, as my mother always says, "Shut up." If you want to find out more about telling your story go to HowToGetASalesJob.com

Pause

A pause is one of the most powerful things that you can do in sales. It is one of the most powerful things that you can do in conversations in general. What happens when you pause? A pause is an indirect probe. You are not probing actively, but you are probing through silence. Try out a pause in a few conversations that you have this week. Just pause after you say something. Do not make an abrupt pause halfway through a sentence. Just finish your thought and then pause. Bite your tongue if you must, and see what happens.

What happens next is amazing. The other person will start to talk. They feel the silence, and they start to talk a lot. If they are not talking, stay silent for another five to ten seconds, and trust me, they will open up. This may feel a bit awkward, but it is a polite way of giving the person the floor to speak. A pause works especially well on the phone. Phone silence is dead airtime, and it is part of the other person's human nature to pick up the conversation.

Why pause now? After interviewing many people over the phone, I find that the biggest problem is that they do not know where, when, or even how to stop talking. If you do not pause, you may spend twelve minutes explaining your excitement about the company. That might put you at 2:20 pm without Sara saying anything.

Over-talking is a terrible way to run a sales call. It demonstrates that you know how to carry a conversation but that you do not know how to share the floor with a prospect. You ramble, and you do not care about the other person's thoughts. If you take away Sara's chance to talk, you are most likely going to take away valuable time from a prospect as well.

There was a VP of Sales who was particularly good at using pauses in conversation. He would ask a question about a deal and then just stop talking. He would ask a sales rep, "What's the latest with Pepsi?" The sales rep would give his or her update on where we are at with the Pepsi account, and then my VP wouldn't say anything.

The rep would keep talking and give him more details about what was going on at Pepsi. The VP would remain quiet. It would get so awkward that the sales rep would just continue providing more and more details about the deal. Eventually, the rep would stop and say, "Are you good with that?" Or sometimes even, "Are you still there?" My VP would say, "Yeah, I am here. Got it, thanks." Talk less on the phone so that other people can talk more. By doing so, they will tell you more.

A pause in a phone interview is really a great tool that you can use. It is perfect for when you finish conveying your excitement. Once you pause, Sara will start talking.

Q&A

A good sales manager will hear you pause and go on to outline the open role, talk a bit about herself and the company, and then begin a natural conversation with you. You have made it to an actual conversation, and this is your chance to shine. You are now able to converse with your potential new boss. Your goal here is to demonstrate that you can answer questions and ask your own questions back to her. This is a course in Human Conversation 101.

This is a bit more free-form and open. I cannot explain what type of questions Sara will ask you. There are many different types of interview styles out there. Typically, a sales manager is trying to probe a bit on a few of the following items:

1. Figure out your character and demeanor

2. Test you (a bit) under pressure

3. Do you have a sense of humor?

4. Behavioral & situational questions

It is difficult to explain to you how to react to any type of hypothetical, situational, or behavioral scenario that Sara may throw your way. It is difficult because of the range of topics or methods that she can use. However, this is similar to any potential sales call that you are going to have in the future. Prospects are a wild card over the phone, and Sara will be too. A prospect could randomly ask you about the support or warranty for your product. They could ask you for an elevator pitch. They could ask you for information about your CEO. There could be a thousand possible scenarios, and it is impossible to prepare for all of them. So, what do you do? What can you possibly do to be prepared for this part of the call?

You could research different interview questions and techniques for preparing appropriately. However, the experts are going to teach you things that will not help you answer questions. They are not going to teach you how to accomplish your only goal on this call - to secure an in-person interview. That is what I will teach you.

One of the best reps I know told me that the most difficult interview question he ever came across was when I asked him, "What are you doing this weekend?"

It was difficult because he had not prepared for it. He did not rehearse his answer, and he did not even think it would come up in an interview. I was successful in throwing him off, and no expert had tipped him off on how to answer my question.

I asked him this because I wanted to see how normal he was. I also asked it because it is just the type of question a prospect might ask. If you have a phone call with a customer on a Friday, one of the first things that they will ask you is, "What are you doing this weekend?" There is no right answer to this. You just have to be honest.

This type of random questioning may come in many forms. Perhaps Sara has seen that you listed mountain biking on your resume, and she asks you about it. Maybe she asks your current salary or what your greatest achievement was.

The guidance from me on these types of random questions is to open up a bit and show authenticity with some excitement. These questions are not meant to explain why you are good at sales. I once asked someone, "What do you like to do after work?" They told me that they liked to study their calls from the day and develop more business plans for the morning. That's fine if you do like that stuff—but it isn't very interesting. If you ever told a prospect this, I am sure that you will not have much in common with them.

I am guilty of this as well. A VP asked me, "what do you like to do for fun?" I wasn't prepared for that question because I was too focused on explaining how good I was at sales. I told him that I like to travel, and that was the extent of my response. He looked at me strangely because it was such a canned answer. (It was.) I hadn't prepared to talk about my life at all. I was just trying to explain that I can achieve my forecast and drive new sales.

I was lucky enough to catch myself quickly and followed it with, "I am actually a big Tom Brady fan. The New England Patriots are my team. My brother and I have been to at least fifty games." The VP immediately started talking about his favorite soccer team. He saw that I had another normal side to me, and we had broken the ice a bit. Don't be boring or canned when faced with any type of random questions. It is okay to be human on this part of the call.

Outside of random or personal questions, the phone call could also go in another direction. Sara could try to test you a bit with questions that are intended to be difficult or even impossible to answer. She is trying to see how you handle a bit of stress. It is important here not to get too agitated or out of focus. Remain calm and focus on providing an answer. This can come in many forms as well.

Examples questions might be:

- Define the word integrity.

- What would your friends say about you?

- Explain how to ride a bike in three sentences or less.

These are random yet potential questions that help interviewers judge how a candidate handles difficult questions. When you are on the phone with a prospect, they are unlikely to ask random and difficult questions, but they could. The only difference between a prospect asking you difficult questions and Sara asking you difficult questions is that Sara is doing it on purpose. A prospect might do it out of pure curiosity. Sara is doing it to see how you would handle that difficult prospect. You may see a connection in the Q&A. Try not to get too hung up on your answers but focus more on how you behave. How you handle yourself in this Q&A is your way of demonstrating to Sara how you will handle yourself in a conversation with a prospect.

Your demeanor is paramount on the call. **It is important not to get frustrated with Sara.** Do not be judgmental about her questioning. Never ask her, "Why are you asking me that?" By doing this, you are putting up a defense mechanism, and it shows very poorly over the phone. I hope that you would never ask a prospect why they are asking you something. It is essential to remain calm and collected at all times while on the phone. If you feel like you are getting a bit flustered with questioning, try to focus on how you can provide Sara with a solid answer that keeps the conversation flowing. The same applies to sales. If a prospect is invasive with questioning, you must remain collected and maintain the flow of the conversation. It is funny to me how many sales rep tell me that they are good at relationships, and then I see them blow a phone interview because they lost their cool. You are in sales. It is your responsibility to maintain a healthy conversation that keeps moving forward.

Let's look at the bullet point above, which asks to explain how to ride a bike in three sentences less. I ask this a lot in interviews. Here are some ways it usually plays out:

I will ask the candidate, "Can you please explain to me how to ride a bike in three sentences or less?"

Before you read on, think about how you would react to this question and how you would answer. Both your reaction and answer are important.

A good candidate will pause and then respond like this.

"In order to ride a bike, you will want to stand it upright and put one leg over the seat with your foot on the pedal. Next, you will push off your foot that is still on the ground and balance the bike while pedaling. Continue to pedal until the bike is moving forward."

That is a perfect answer because the candidate followed my directions. The candidate understood what I was asking and explained the answer. There is much more involved when riding a bike, but this candidate demonstrates that they can simply follow directions. In a sales cycle, I am going to need a rep who can follow my directions. I will also need someone who can answer a prospect's questions without getting defensive. This quality will ultimately lead to better sales calls with prospects, which will lead to more revenue for the company. It also shows that I have a rep who listens.

Below average candidates will answer my question like this:

(Laughing) "Why do you want to know that? You don't know how to ride a bike?"

"Three sentences? That is tough. How do you want me to do it? Who am I explaining this to? What do people usually say when you ask them this?"

Or my favorite, "Why?"

Every one of these reactions is bad. It may seem acceptable in a scenario if you were talking to your friend, but in a phone interview, a sales manager is asking you difficult questions intentionally so they can see how you react. They are trying to push your buttons and these reactions without directly answering demonstrate how you will act in the future with prospects. In each of these responses, the candidate never gave an answer. They just reacted apprehensively.

Any type of reaction like this in a phone interview clearly shows defensiveness, a lack of trust, inability to understand simple directions, hesitation, misunderstanding of a situation, and slow comprehension. It is okay to react that way in public but not in a sales interview.

In other scenarios, I will push strong candidates a bit further and ask them, "When is your birthday?" I'll ask them this right in the middle of them explaining how to ride a bike.

A lot of candidates will pause and ask, "Why?" Some will laugh at me make fun of me for asking the question. Whereas the best candidates will rattle off an answer, "February 21st," and then keep explaining how to ride a bike.

If a prospect asked you to explain something and then halfway through your explanation, they asked you a random question, would you laugh at them and ask why they asked that? No. So why would you do this with a sales manager in a phone interview? **Candidates have reactions like this all the time in interviews because of stress and nerves.** The sales managers do this on purpose. They want you to buckle under pressure and become defensive and aggravated. If you do this, you will be hurting your chances of advancing.

As a sales manager, following directions is an important skill for a sales rep to have, and that is why I ask candidates to explain a specific how-to. It is important to me and a good measuring stick. To other sales managers, like Sara Jones, they will have their own skillsets that they see as important, so their line of questioning could be anything. It might be anything like, "What kind of ice cream do you like?" to, "If you had a million dollars, what would you do with it?"

You do not have to prepare for every single question. You can't. Google is famous for asking nearly impossible questions to see candidates' reactions. It is important to understand all of this and to know that your only goal in a phone interview is to answer questions professionally and keep the conversation moving. Never take yourself too seriously or get defensive during a Q&A. You can always ask for clarification but just be sure to answer Sara's questions. She has her own reasons for asking them.

Never lie about anything. I have interviewed a thousand people, and if you are lying about something, I can tell. Other managers will also be able to decipher lies over the phone. Our job is to cut through the nonsense and assess difficult situations. We have a knack for calling bluffs, and it is the absolute worst quality to have as a sales rep.

Even if a question is going to expose you, it is important to own it and tell the truth.

I was once asked in an interview to outline the cube technology related to the product I'd be selling. The best thing I ever did was respond with, "I'm not sure what that is. What do you mean by cube technology?"

After the interview, I was hired. The manager told me that I was the only candidate who was honest about not knowing more about the underlying technology. He said that all the candidates pretended to know it, and that's not what he was looking for. He was looking for a sales rep, not a product expert. Managers are hiring you for your ability to sell. No one is hiring you based on your product knowledge.

Product knowledge is a common topic that candidates ask about. If a candidate is interviewing at Microsoft, they will ask how to learn about all the products before the phone interview. Microsoft sells thousands of products. There is no possible way to learn all the products. Microsoft hires people to be product experts. They are looking to hire you to conduct a sales process. If you are a sales rep at Microsoft and a customer asks you about technical requirements and you do not know, just tell them that you do not know. It is okay. You are in sales and not a product manager. Explain that you don't know because you are just the sales rep, and then introduce them to the people that know the answer.

Most sales reps know to avoid questions they do not know on a sales call, so I do not know why they love to pretend to answer them during a phone interview. It might be stress, but I think it is because they are taught the dos and don'ts of a sales process and never taught the dos and don'ts of a sales job application process.

It is fair to say that most of the Q&A on a phone interview can be difficult, confusing, nerve-racking, and lengthy. The key takeaways are to stay focused and calm, answer the questions at hand, be concise, and keep the conversation moving.

A moving conversation means that you should never give an answer that lasts longer than twenty seconds. If you find yourself talking too much, take a deep breath, finish up your answer, and stop talking. Trust me. If you are trying to get into sales, you may enjoy talking. It is okay to be talkative, but if you are using one to three minutes for each answer during a Q&A on your phone interview, you are not conducting a proper call, and you might ruin your chances of securing an in-person interview.

Next Step & Ask For An In-Person

When you are talking to a friend or family member on the phone, you rarely pay attention to the time. However, during a phone interview, timing is critical. Sara Jones may very well be quietly observing your time management skills. She will want to understand if you can run a call within the allotted time and how you react if it is going overboard.

At this point on a strongly run call, the time should be close to 2:22 pm. If you have been talking too much, it might be closer to 2:28 pm or 2:29 pm, and you are basically out of time. If that's the case, you have clearly demonstrated that you can't hold an effective thirty-minute sales call. What's even worse is that you will only have about a minute left to finalize the next steps. This is suboptimal, and I highly recommend not getting within the threshold of a couple of minutes left when you do try to close the call.

If you notice it is 2:25 pm or later and you still have a Q&A, this is a poorly run sales call, and you need to cut your losses. You may think it is awesome that Sara wants to talk to you for so long. I don't care if every expert on planet Earth tells you that the longer the call, the better. They are all wrong. The point of a thirty-minute phone interview is to talk briefly about your story, answer a couple of questions, and schedule an in-person interview.

Most sales managers will be observing your time management. Even if they keep you talking, it could be a tactic to see if you have the ability and authority to stop the call and point out the timing. Timing is important on sales calls. This is your phone call, which means it is up to you to keep track.

Most sales managers will see it as a very positive quality if you point out that at 2:22 pm, you are almost out of time and you would like to discuss the next steps. Eight minutes is not a lot of time, and Sara may have another call set for 2:30 pm. Your indication of the time is very polite and gives her a solid look at how respectful you would be on sales calls with prospects. By running your phone interview this way, you will have ample time to close Sara, and it also leaves less time for questioning. This will work to your benefit every time.

Let's move forward with the idea that you ran the call properly, and it is now 2:22 pm. You point out that you are almost at the thirty-minute mark and defer to Sara. She may finish with, "So, what questions do you have for me?"

This is typically a good indicator that you are on the right path. Tread carefully. Most candidates still tend to screw up the call even after the sales manager opens the floor for questions. How do they screw it up?

By asking the wrong question. By asking too many questions. By not asking any questions at all.

When you are asked if you have any questions, the sales manager is inviting you to close out the conversation. You had your fun with greetings and introductions. You shared your story and followed up with a healthy (but short) Q&A. It is time to end it by asking if you can meet them for an in-person interview. For most candidates, this is the most difficult thing to ask. Typically, candidates shy away from this question and instead use this time as a forum for asking questions that would be better suited for an in-person conversation.

I have seen candidates ace the first part of the phone interview, and then when I ask them if they have any questions, they ask me things like, "What do you think about your company's profit and loss ratio and how it compares to trends in the market?" That's a good question. But honestly, I have never met you face to face, and we have a few minutes left to discuss our next steps. Is this really what's at the front of mind for you?

Or I'll hear, "What do sales reps typically wear in your office?", "What's the salary?" "Do you like your job?" "What type of 30-60-90-day plan do you expect?"

You did not go through the hard work of building a resume, targeting companies, making contact, and setting up a phone interview only to close out the final minutes of your precious phone interview by discussing the company's P&L or, even worse, the dress code.

You only need to ask Sara two questions. The first question should focus on asking Sara her thoughts about you as a candidate or if she has any concerns. Asking for her validation is what a professional sales rep would do.

The second question you should ask is, "Can we schedule some time for me to come in and meet you in-person?"

Sara wants you to ask this too, but she's not going to tell you that. She wants to see how you will set it up. When you are speaking with a prospect on the phone, and they give you an opening, it is always best to ask for an in-person meeting. Would you ever ask a prospect about their P&L trends with 2 minutes to go in your first call? Absolutely not.

Sara asks, "So, what questions do you have for me?"

"Well, my goal is to get some time on your calendar for an in-person interview, so I just want to know if you have any initial concerns with me as a candidate?"

It is particularly important to ask Sara this question. It sends out a tone of confidence and it gives you a chance to defend any issues she may have. If you never ask her this question, you will never know where she stands. Clarifying where she stands gives you the chance to defend yourself.

If you ask this question, Sara will either tell you, "I see no obstacles." Or she will tell you, "I have some concerns about

XYZ." No obstacles? You are in the clear. Move on to the final question and ask to meet in person. But if she has some reservations, this is your one opportunity to address them.

While you should absolutely defend yourself and your abilities, never get defensive. I once asked for validation, and the manager said, "It seems like you are too much of an individual and not much a team player." I responded by asking if it was okay to elaborate on the topic of teamwork, and he let me. This manager later told me that he was testing me to see if I was going to stand up for myself or get defensive. **Managers really do try to test candidates during phone interviews**. It is important to be aware of that, and you must project yourself as a confident sales professional at all times.

Obstacles, concerns, or reservations can come in any form. Maybe Sara will say that she does not think you have sales experience or, more commonly, she does not think that you have *enough* sales experience. If the question about *enough* sales experience comes up, you owe it to yourself to point out all the transferable, sales-related skills you possess and tell her very clearly that you are *coachable*.

This instantly shows you know what sales skills are (since you have performed them in some capacity before), and secondly, it shows that with the right coach (or manager), you are willing to learn and can be successful. A good sales manager will love this and want to take you under their wing. A bad sales manager will want you to go work for IBM for eleven years before you get the job. (But you do not want to work for bad sales managers, so it is okay.)

Being able to point out sales-related skills and being coachable is huge when it comes to hiring someone without enough prior sales experience. Remember that sales-related skills are all of those sales-related activities that we identified earlier in my process. There is no arguing the fact that you have performed sales-related activities. You just have to speak to them clearly now.

Addressing the question of a lack of experience might look like this:

"While I don't have experience carrying a quota, I have performed sales-related activities such as cold calling and emailing prospects at other organizations. Once I learn your sales process from you, I will be able to put it into play. I am coach-able and just need the opportunity to prove this to you."

Make this paragraph your own by adding your personal objectives: you have performed sales activities before, and you are coachable. End with telling them you just need that opportunity. No need to go on an endless rant. Short and direct. After this, it is time for your final question.

Before I got into sales, I always heard about "closing." I had heard a lot about it (as I am sure you have too). I knew that people closed on houses. Baseball pitchers closed out games. In movies like *Boiler Room* and *The Wolf of Wall Street*, the sales reps are always talking about closing. You have probably heard people mention the famous sales phrase, "ABC," which translates to "Always Be Closing."

For me, closing scared me to death. I pictured it as this huge engagement you had to take hours to prepare for, in a board room. I wondered how somebody closed somebody else in real life. Was it some type of formal discussion? Is there a document involved? How do you start a close? How does a close end? I had no clue. It turned out to be nothing like that.

The Close

I am not going to lie; closing can be tough for people. But it is only tough if you make it tough. If you mentally make closing out to be some big event in your mind, you may be missing the point of what a close actually is.

Closing is a simple and direct ask for something that you want. My first time closing someone was when I was seven years old. I remember asking my parents if I finished my homework before dinner, would they let me ride bikes with my neighbor? They agreed. I had successfully closed two middle-aged, rational people at seven years old.

You close someone by asking for a yes or no response regarding something you want from them.

"Will you marry me?" A closing question.

"Can we go to McDonald's for lunch?" Another one.

You probably close people ten times a day without noticing. Now, all you must do is close Sara Jones over the phone, and you are golden.

The most traditional way to close someone on a phone interview is to use an "if/ then" statement. "If I do this, then will you let me do this…" An "if/ then" is the oldest and most traditional close. I am a big fan because it is so straightforward.

Some of you are probably thinking, *So, I just have to use an "if, then" statement with Sara? That sounds easy.*

It is easy. But do you know why it is so difficult and one of the most nerve-racking things that you can ask someone? It's because there is a chance that the other person will say no.

Will you marry me?

No.

Ouch.

Do you see how painful a close can be? It can hurt your ego, and it could send you on a downward spiral. I totally understand. Asking for an in-person interview and getting denied can be heart-wrenching. It happens to the best of us. It has happened to me a few times, but there is an underlying benefit in rejection.

The benefit is that you have your answer. You know where you stand. Whether it is a yes or a no, you know where you stand with someone after you ask a proper closing question. By knowing where you stand with someone, you will save yourself time – which is extremely valuable.

Right now, there are thousands of sales candidates sitting around by the phone, waiting to hear back on a job. This prevents you from moving forward with your job search, and it all stems from not closing the sales manager

As a rep, you would find yourself in the same situation, sitting around by the phone, if you ended a prospect call with, "Okay, have a nice day. Hope to hear from you soon."

By not closing Sara, you have no idea where you stand with her. I have seen this happen a hundred times, and this is usually how it plays out:

While you are waiting around for her to call you, you remain hopeful and let a few days go by. Then a couple of weeks. Suddenly, it is a month later since you last spoke to her. You check with a friend who asks you, "Well, what's the next step?" Panic sets in as you reply with, "I'm not sure."

You start sending emails to her. Only now, you are trying to close her in your emails because you realize that you do not know where you stand, and you have no confirmed next steps.

You shoot them off carelessly with phrases like, "Please let me know when is best to connect next." Or worse, "I'd like to know if you have any concerns with me as a candidate." You are trying to close her a month later—via email!

If you waste your time, you will regret it. If you waste Sara's time, she will remember you are not a closer. Sounds ruthless? It's true.

The funniest part about all of this is that you could have avoided all of this wasted time and instead closed Sara with one sentence.

"If you are okay with it, can we set up a time in-person to talk more about the job?"

That's it… that's your big scary closing statement. If you ask it, you are going to see faster, better results, and you will ultimately save time in your search. You are going to get a YES or a NO right away from Sara.

If you get a no… guess what? Remember those A, B, and C-lists filled with a list of contacts? It is time to move on to the next target company on your list and continue following my process. You will save yourself a lot of time and energy and you may even find a better fit. You may also get some great feedback from Sara as to why you are not a fit, and you can adjust your approach with the next interview.

If Sara replies, "Yes, that sounds good to me." **You are all set.** Book the interview with her and get a firm next step on date and time. She may have to follow up by email, and if that's the case, you are still okay. Once she responds positively to your ask for an in-person interview, you just have to work on the administrative part of setting that meeting up.

You might also experience a soft yes from Sara. What is a soft yes? If Sara says something like, "Sure. Let me follow up with my admin, and she'll reach out to schedule an interview in-person." That's a soft yes. You technically have a next step defined, but it is not 100% written in stone. This is very typical, and it is okay in my book as long as you have the verbal commitment from her.

Don't be aggressive and push relentlessly to schedule the in-person meeting while on the phone with her. Do not say things like, "Okay, can you please ask her now and open your calendar? I'd like to set it up now before we get off the phone." I have had people do this to me, and it is just way too pushy. It was almost as if they did not trust me. I would never want them acting so aggressively with a prospect.

You do not need a hard close on the phone. You just need Sara's verbal commitment that she will get it done. You have been direct and accurate in defining the next step. The next step is that her admin will reach out. Mission accomplished. Take a deep breath and politely end the call.

If you are unsure if you have accomplished the goal, try to think about it this way. When someone asks you, "What's the next step?" If you can tell them what that step is, you have accomplished the goal. "She's going to have her admin reach out to set up the in-person interview." You did it.

Let's recap the close.

You closed Sara by asking her if she had any concerns. She did not. Then you asked her to set up an in-person interview. She agreed. At this point, you are probably close to 2:30 pm. Time to end it. How? Confirm, restate, thank her, goodbye. Do not linger. Lingering is the worst.

Try something like this, "Okay, Sara. That's perfect. So, you are going to email your admin and set up a time. I'll wait to hear from her?" Let Sara answer positively. Then follow with, "Great, thank you so much. I look forward to it. Have a good day and talk to you soon." She'll say thank you and goodbye, and then you say bye and end it. Do not make this go on and on. If you find yourself wanting to end the call and that you may be lingering a bit too much, you are too late. You are lingering. If you are feeling this, she is 100% already feeling too. You have made the sale; end it. Her time is valuable too.

If you have followed my process correctly, you can take a look at your watch and see that it is now somewhere between 2:29 and 2:30 pm. If you have gone over (even by a couple of minutes), you must be critical of yourself so that you can increase your self-awareness. Think about why you ran over and next time you have a phone interview, work hard to tighten it up.

But you did make it through with Sara. Nice job. Now what?

Thank You Notes

Go to Google and search for, "Should you send a thank-you note after an interview?" You will see thousands of articles, blogs, discussions, and forums on this question. The reason it is so highly debated is that there are many progressive experts in sales who like going against the traditional answer. (Which is yes, you should.) Some of these experts think that to command respect or show your authority; you do not have to send a thank-you note. This is a terrible strategy.

Never, in the history of the world, has a thank-you note hurt a candidate's chances of moving forward. Therefore, as a best practice, you should send a thank-you note if you want to move forward.

1. If Sara is expecting one, you are golden.

2. If Sara is not expecting one, you have done extra credit.

3. If Sara is going to be annoyed that you sent one, you have lost the job.

The good news here is that the third scenario is unrealistic. If you want to argue that it could happen, I would argue that if that's truly the case, you are in a better position because you do not want to work for someone who gets upset about thank-you notes.

To connect it back to an actual sales process, let's pretend it is a prospect. You just had a great phone call with a prospect, and send a thank-you note. The prospect gets angry and does not want to do business with you. Does this seem realistic? No.

I have worked with experienced candidates who told me they do not send thank-you notes because it makes them look weak. Then I ask them if they would send a thank-you note to the CFO at one of their prospects after a meeting. They immediately say yes. Sometimes, they even send a gift basket to that company's office. If you are doing it with prospects, why would you not do it with potential employers? It is the same concept. Just don't send Sara a gift basket – that's overkill.

Your thank-you note does not have to be lengthy, but it does have to be sent out with a tone of respect. A sales manager just spent thirty minutes with you when they could have spent thirty minutes doing a million other things. They could have been managing a deal, working on a contract, updating a forecast, or even talking to another candidate. If you do not send a thank-you note, you are going to be considered disrespectful.

You should send a thank-you note anywhere from thirty-minutes to ten hours after your phone interview. Some candidates wait until the next day to avoid seeming overly eager, but in my experience, it is best to keep it short and sweet and click send the same day.

If you wait until the next day, you may end up just hurting your chances. I have asked some sales managers how a phone interview went, and they have said, "I talked to her yesterday, but I haven't heard anything from her since." I have never once heard a sales manager say, "Well, I interviewed her this morning, and she immediately sent a thank-you note. I typically like to see candidates wait an entire day to send one. She seems too eager for me." This never happens! If you think like this, it is probably because you have heard bad advice from one of those "experts" out there.

Send a thank-you note within ten hours that day and keep it short. I say ten hours because sometimes you have to go back to work or real life just gets in the way. Ten hours is considered the same day. Any longer, and you are pushing it. The thank-you note should be in the form of an email, and it should only be two to three sentences max. Anything longer is overkill.

Try something like the following:

> Hi Sara,
>
> Thank you for your time this afternoon. I really enjoyed our conversation, and I am excited about the opportunity. I look forward to hearing from your admin next week, and please feel free to reach out if you have any questions.
>
> Best,
>
> John

If you would like more thank you note examples go to HowToGetASalesJob.com

What did you just do there? You thanked Sara for her time. It is reiterated that you are excited about the opportunity. You have expressed that you are looking forward to the next step. Make sure you also check for spelling. I have received misspelled thank-you notes, and it just puts a damper on things. Make the subject of your email "Thank You" and click Send.

Here is where my process increases your chances exponentially versus what you may have done in the past. You are not done with thank-you notes yet.

What else do you have to do? What is going to separate you from the fifteen other candidates applying for this open sales job? Not many people do this, but it is a big part of my process, and it works wonders.

You need to send a "Thank You" to every gatekeeper that you interacted with during the process. For example, if your former colleague introduced you to the executive admin and this executive admin helped coordinate your phone interview with Sara Jones, you must send a thank you note to both your former colleague and the executive admin.

Or perhaps, you spoke to a recruiter, and they put you in touch with a current sales rep. Then that sales rep connected you to a VP of Sales. After you spoke with the VP of Sales, they put you in touch with Sara Jones. In this scenario, you must send a thank-you note to the recruiter, the current sales rep, and the VP of Sales. Always include a thank-you note for Sara Jones in every scenario, and do not forget the others who helped along the way

Each thank-you notes can be framed in a similar way. These examples always work best.

> Hi Gatekeeper,
>
> Thank you so much for setting me up with Sara. I just finished speaking with her, and it went very well. I am expecting to hear back from her admin next week regarding an in-person interview. Thank you again for the time. I am excited about the opportunity.
> Best,
> John

Why should you do this? Why do you send thank you notes to everyone you spoke with throughout the process? You do this because it is next-level selling. You are proactively spreading the news that your phone interview went well while at the same time expressing gratitude and excitement to others throughout the organization.

Let's pretend that the admin goes for coffee later that day with Sara. When they are waiting in line at Starbucks, there is a high probability that the admin could say something like, "How did it go with John? He sent me a thank-you note as well. He's so nice!" That one comment goes a long way. It goes longer than you think. This comment may just be the reassurance that Sara was looking for.

Never forget the people who helped you set up the phone interview. Their input matters. When I was a manager, I asked every one of my colleagues who spoke to the candidate over the phone what they were thinking. Many sales managers do this. It is especially useful to hear what others in your company think about the potential new rep. Not many candidates send multiple thank-you notes. If you do this, you will be ahead of the pack. It could also be the start of a great working relationship with your future coworkers. In fact, if all goes well, you will be working with these gatekeepers soon.

Thank-you notes sent. Now what? Congratulations – you are moving on to a sales interview.

Chapter 8: In-Person Interview

Stanley Kubrick's film, *The Shining*, opens with a scene titled, 'The Interview.' In this scene, Jack Torrance (played by Jack Nicholson) is applying for a job to be the overseer of a remote hotel up in the mountains. The scene begins with Nicholson greeting a receptionist in the lobby, followed by a long walk together through creepy hallways that only Kubrick could make you appreciate. Nicholson makes his way into an office where he is greeted by a creepy old man. They shake hands and Nicholson sits down for the interview, crossing his legs, and providing his trademark smile. He isn't wearing Versace or Prada, but he is dressed in a suit and tie. The back-and-forth of the interview is cordial and traditional; nothing out of the ordinary.

Suddenly, the conversation takes a chilling turn. The old man explains that the person who previously had this job had hacked his entire family up with an ax and then froze to death in the woods. Nicholson makes a quick joke and then reassures the interviewer that even though it sounds like a tragedy, he sees no problem with this affecting his ability to do the job. He finishes with why he's the best fit for the job and closes the interview by getting the job offer.

It is unsettling because the audience knows this is a horror movie and how it will play out. Yet, the interview itself is worth reviewing.

While it is not a sales interview, it does highlight two important things for every hopeful sales candidate. **First, if you are going in for an interview, your main goal is to get a job offer.** Regardless of anything else, this is your mission. **Secondly, when you are in the interview, you must be ready for anything they throw at you.**

Crazy things can happen during an interview, but focusing on this goal will help you stay on track even if they tell you that the previous sales rep hacked his family to death with an ax. That doesn't apply to your situation, and you are still interested in moving forward in the process. It sounds dramatic, but I trust you see my point.

If you find yourself turning down a job during the interview, you may miss out on other opportunities. Once, I was in an interview, and halfway through, I realized that I did not want the job. But I put that thought aside and focused on my goal of getting a job offer. Afterward, I received a call from the sales manager, who let me know that I was overqualified for this role, but he offered me a different job within the company. Had I turned down the initial job during the interview, this other opportunity never would have happened. The point is, even if you are not 100% interested during the interview, it does not matter. Act like Nicholson. Smile and close the interviewer anyway.

You are about to have an in-person interview with Sara Jones. It is time to shine. A lot of experts consider the in-person interview to be the most important part of the entire job application process. This is the one time when I'll agree with the experts. The interview is the most important part, but it is not the hardest part. The hardest part of a sales job application process is getting your foot in the door. Once you are in the door, the interview becomes vital because you only have one chance to meet in-person. If you do cannot execute in-person, your opportunity will vanish.

4 Keys

If you remember anything about my process, please remember that during an in-person interview, you must accomplish these four key items in order to have the best chance of receiving a job offer.

1.   The Interviewer needs to like you.

2.   The Interviewer needs to remember you.

3.   The Interviewer needs to vouch for you to their Manager.

4.   You need to secure the next steps.

Many candidates think this sounds easy, but none of this is easy, especially not the first three items. Sales candidates think that the easy part of an interview is getting someone to like them and remember them. In reality, this is extremely difficult because it involves a lot of intangibles.

Many candidates I have interviewed will talk about the weather, sports, or traffic and assume that if I agree that traffic is horrendous, the weather is nice, and the Patriots are a good team, it means that I like them. That's simply not true. These things are all superficial to me. I like honest people, and I like confident people. How would I know that these candidates are honest and confident if they just talk about things like the weather? I wouldn't.

The worst part is that these candidates would leave my office under the assumption that I like them. Liking someone is subjective, which makes it difficult to assess. We are all guilty of thinking people like us because we simply want it to be true. However, accomplishing this feat is difficult. I can't help you out in everyday life, but I can tell you how to get people to like you and remember you during an in-person sales interview.

Let's start by having you think about your best friend. This could be someone from high school, maybe your college roommate, your neighbor, your cousin – you know who it is. Think about that person who you can be your full and honest self around. This is the person you can call and talk to for hours and always find something to laugh about. Think about the person you want to sit next to at parties or spend your free time with.

While thinking about your best friend, I want you to think about how you greet them when you see them. Think about that initial embrace. Typically, it will involve something like this… You smile, slap hands, hug, laugh, bring up something the two of you have in common, and try to make each other smile. Picture it now: it is genuine, warm, and welcoming. It feels comfortable.

What would the opposite of that interaction look like?

If you saw your best friend, walked up to them quietly and coldly put out your hand for a formal handshake and said, "Hi." Or perhaps even, "Hello. How are you?" How would they receive your greeting? They would instantly look at you concerned and think, "What's wrong?"

Why is your greeting important in this situation if you are not about to meet your best friend? You are about to meet Sara Jones. You haven't known her for as long, so why does it matter?

If you get this sales job, you are going to be spending a lot of time with Sara. You may even become close friends with her and work together for many years. In the long run, we tend to spend more time at work than with our families and friends.

If things work out, you will be working for Sara and making money for yourself and making money for her. So, if you initially approach her with a hand extended and say, "Hello," "Hi," "Hey," or anything dry like this, you are setting yourself up to fail.

Sara will immediately think to herself,

"Uh-oh, what's wrong? Why is this person being cold?"

"Where is their passion and excitement--their energy?"

"What happens when I bring this person to my VP, and they greet him flatly like this? I can't hire this person."

I know this seems dramatic. So many thoughts are running through Sara's mind from only a handshake and hello. But this is how real-life works. This is why people believe in love at first sight. This is why you've always been told that a first impression is everything. **A first impression is not the sixty minutes you spend with Sara. A first impression is made in the first two seconds that you spend with Sara.** It is extremely important and could be the deciding factor.

If you fail on this initial interaction, it won't matter how good your 30-60-90 business plan is. (Tip: you will not be providing a 30-60-90.) If you fail in your initial interaction with Sara, nothing else will matter as much. It is a weighted average, and your first impression is weighted the most. You have no chance of Sara liking you if she does not feel comfortable right off the bat.

I will now run through how a successful sales interview should play out. By covering each step along the way, we'll naturally incorporate the four key items and ensure you execute a successful interview.

Logistics

First things first. Where are you going? Which building? Is it on the third floor or the eighth? Is it an office or a coffee shop? Is there parking on-site, or will you have to bring money for the meter?

It is your job to figure out the logistics. This is highly underrated, and many candidates ignore it. Do yourself a favor and assess the site. If the interview is in a place that you are extremely familiar with, there is no need to do this. However, if you are not 100% sure what the site of the interview is like, you must go do some recon. The military does recon in order to ensure they are overly prepared for any situation. You should too. This is a big day for you.

I suggest doing your recon the day before. This will give you time to plan ahead. If you cannot visit the site before the big day, plan to arrive at least forty-five minutes early. Factor in traffic, parking, flat tires, etc. and do whatever it takes to ensure you arrive forty-five minutes early.

This will give you plenty of time to familiarize yourself with the situation and with your surroundings. By doing so, you will be able to handle any surprises, and you will decrease any risk of being late.

I once showed up for an interview ten minutes early. About five minutes before the interview was supposed to start, the receptionist said, "Oh wait, it is actually in the other Tower. I am sorry, I forgot to mention that." I stood up and panicked. I started running towards the other Tower. I showed up out of breath and off my game.

Had I arrived forty-five minutes earlier, maybe the receptionist would have reminded me I was in the wrong tower with more time to spare. I could have avoided this problem and walked over at a normal pace.

That's an example of a surprise. Surprises can still happen regardless of how early you arrive, but if you are forty-five minutes early, you have a better chance of handling them.

The second reason for being so early is that you never want to be late. I have come across articles where so-called experts claim that it is okay to be late to an interview if you have a good reason because your time is just as valuable.

To avoid any confusion – that is simply not true in sales.

Time management is everything. If you show up late to your interview, you are demonstrating that you will show up late to a sales meeting with a prospect. What if that prospect were the CFO or CIO? It doesn't matter who it is – they're not going to buy anything from you if you're late.

Showing up late for an interview means you will not get the job. This is a job where you must consistently show up for meetings and ask prospects to spend money with you. **If you are late for a sales interview with me, Sara Jones, or any other sales manager on planet Earth, you will not get the job.**

It should be common sense that if you arrive this early, it is not necessary to go sit in the lobby awkwardly and stare at the clock. You can wait in your car or outside the building without making a scene. The goal is to be early, but you never want to be that person lingering too long before the interview. If you feel like you're in the right spot, wait until 15 minutes beforehand, and then you can head into the lobby.

Resumes

Find out how many people you will be meeting with, and then plan to bring two more hard copies of your resume than that number. If you are scheduled to meet with five people, you should bring seven resumes. Bring extra in case another person joins the meeting unexpectedly or in case you spill coffee on a copy. Having a couple of extra resumes is always better.

If you are reluctant to bring a hard copy of your resume with you to a sales interview, think about risk versus reward. There is no way that bringing resumes can hurt you. However, there are at least fifteen ways that a missing resume could hurt you. What if you do not bring a copy of your resume because you want to be digital, and then a 60-year-old EVP of Sales shows up and says, "Do you have a copy of your resume?" If you say no, you just lost a point.

Even if you claim that you are high-tech and sent a soft copy, he may be old school and not appreciate it. It would be similar to showing up to a sales meeting without any relevant material about your product. You do not need to lead by handing out a hard copy of your resume. You can keep it in your bag, but you must be prepared if they ask for it. Remember, my process is all about best practice.

John P. Davis

A Pen, Notebook & Notes

Bring something to write with. I never write anything down anymore. I usually type things on my phone or laptop. But I have been in many sales interviews where a very casual question comes up where the interviewer wants to draw up a scenario, and they ask, "Do you have a pen?" It will not kill your chance of moving forward if you say no, but it is much better to say, "Yes, here you go," and then pass them the pen. It shows that you are prepared.

It is also a good idea to bring a small notebook. You can pick up a standard notebook at Staples for $3. You do not need more than this, but it is a good idea to have on hand in case you need to write something down. Get something simple and keep it in your bag. I worked for a sales executive who firmly believed in taking notes during a meeting with a prospect.

There is a professional way to take notes that shows you are writing down important items to remember without appearing like a reporter. It is a delicate balance. You must not pull out a notebook five seconds into the meeting and start writing down everything that the interviewer says. You should aim to keep your notebook and pen easily accessible and reach for it when you feel the instinct that what the interviewer is telling you is important to remember.

An unimportant detail to write down would be anything related to the products or services. That material is too technical and meant to be discussed, not studied. The best option is to take notes sparingly towards the end of the interview when important next step details are being discussed. Where do you keep your pen and your notebook? In your bag.

Your Bag

Should you bring a briefcase? How about a backpack, or perhaps just a purse or satchel? How about nothing at all? When it comes to your bag choice, just be yourself. Try not to call too much attention to your bag. It should be one that easily stores your laptop, a small notebook, a pen, a few resumes, and other small items.

Do not bring a backpack. You will look like a college student. This is not the best practice. There are reps who think it is okay, but all it takes is one sales manager who thinks you look like a college student, and you have lost a step.

I recommend any type of laptop bag in traditional business colors of either black, brown, or navy. You should be able to carry this type of bag in one hand, and it will be fine for any type of sales job interview. You do not want any kind of fancy design that draws too much attention. Remember, we are limiting details that can unnecessarily deduct points from you as a candidate. Vibrant colors could be a factor.

Aesthetics and Extras

Bring a charger for your phone and one for your laptop. Do not charge your phone or laptop during the interview, but it is important to have the chargers in case you need it.

If you wear contact lenses, bring an extra pair. You do not want to be blind in one eye if you get dust in your contact three minutes before the interview. You can always run to the bathroom and change a lens at the last minute. But you can't run home and grab one. Imagine how difficult, distracting, and embarrassing it would be squinting during your interview. This would lead to you making excuses for your appearance or performance during the interview. It is a bad look. Pun intended.

Bring mints. I will typically have a mint on my way into the building. If the interviewer arrives early and I still have it in my mouth, I chew it quickly, so I am not sucking on it while I am in their presence. Do not bring or chew gum at all. This is unprofessional. You would never chew gum in a meeting with a prospect. It is much easier to chew and swallow a mint as opposed to swallowing or spitting out your gum in the lobby.

Check your breath too. A lot of sales reps do not know that they have bad breath. It is not a reason to not hire someone, but if I am an interviewer, I am trying to decide if I want to spend a lot of time with the candidate. I am also trying to decide if our prospects will want to spend time with this person. If their breath smells like kitty litter, I may think twice about hiring them.

Make sure you shower before your interview. People can tell. Nothing more to say on that.

Presentation

There is both art and strategy involved with presenting yourself to a sales manager. The art comes from your clothing and style, while the strategy revolves around your actions, presence, and command. Candidates who are unfamiliar with a sales interview tend to downplay how important it is that they present themselves well. It is natural to think this way when you haven't been in this situation before.

Try to imagine a sales rep going into a prospect's office for the first time. In that initial meeting, it doesn't matter if the prospect *wants* to judge the rep on how they present themselves because it will *happen naturally*. In any environment where a sale could take place, human instincts take over, and people subconsciously assess the person who is attempting the sale. An initial sales meeting will involve much more subconscious judgment than an initial meeting in other environments.

For example, imagine if you went to buy a new car and the sales rep had a big coffee stain on his shirt. Would you be more or less inclined to buy a car from him?

However, if you met with a mechanic and he had a big coffee stain on his shirt, would you be more or less inclined to let him fix your car?

In sales, presentation matters much more because you are trying to sell a product, service, idea, or a luxury. While in other fields, these things don't matter as much. Presentation is key for someone when they are trying to sell a product.

Every single day, the outfit you are wearing speaks volumes, whether this is your intention or not. Sometimes your intentions are clear, and you focus on your presentation that day. This is why women wear bridal gowns on their wedding day. Other times, you have no intention about how you present yourself, such as college students wearing sweatpants on Sunday mornings. Without even thinking about it, the college students are conveying an attitude of laziness that says they want to be left alone to chill. Your outfit speaks volumes about what you are trying to accomplish.

On the day of a sales interview, candidates need to dress with the intent that they have already become a sales rep on Sara's team. A lot of people disagree with me on how to convey this intent but trust me when I tell you that **overdressing is best practice.** There are too many candidates who believe business casual or a casual look is appropriate for a sales interview.

It is true that a lot of sales organizations have a relaxed dress code. Sales reps have become less formal and more relaxed in appearance over the past five to ten years. Since things in the office have become less formal, many candidates believe that this applies to how they should dress for their interview. They are all wrong.

A sales interview is not your average day at the office. You do not have the job yet. You are in a situation where you are deliberately trying to convey your seriousness as a candidate to someone who will be judging your appearance. It is much more formal than you think. It is entirely up to the interviewer to determine what the best and most appropriate dress code is for his or her organization. They may even be okay with you wearing jeans once hired, but you are never going to know any of this before your interview.

Therefore, my process requires a formal dress code for your interview. Women should choose a business-appropriate dress and jacket, or a blazer and blouse paired with a skirt or dress pants. Men should wear a suit and tie. Trust me. I am well aware that you will not be wearing a suit and tie nor a blazer and blouse full-time in the role of a sales rep. I also understand that deep down, you may be concerned that other reps in the office will think you are overdressed for this type of "modern company."

However, after hundreds of interviews, I have concluded that formal outfits will never prevent a candidate from getting the job. They are the safest and most appropriate attire for a sales interview. Formal business attire states that you are serious, polished, and respectful. Respect is the key. It is a sign of respect to dress this way. If you are demonstrating respect in your initial meeting, Sara is going to assume that you will demonstrate that same respect with the prospects you meet.

Other candidates might be thinking, "A tie is uncomfortable, and no one even wears them anymore. I am younger than other candidates, and I want to show that I am more up-to-date with the times by not wearing a tie." When candidates tell me things like this, I have to reiterate that you are just adding unnecessary risk to your interview by thinking this way.

229

I had an experience one time where I wore a tie to an interview and felt very overdressed upon arrival. Then halfway through the interview, the CFO walked by and popped in to introduce himself. The first thing out of his mouth was, "I like your tie." He didn't stay long, but he also wore a tie. Maybe it gave me an edge over someone, maybe not. But it didn't hurt me. There is no specific outfit that you must wear, but for the best results, dress formally for an interview. It shows respect, prepares you for anyone you might run into, and it will never hurt you.

If a sales manager ever asks you, "Why so formal?" It is easy to joke about how excited you were and how you wanted to clean up for the first meeting. A good sales manager will appreciate it and never hold it against you.

Carrying yourself in a confident manner should go without saying. It's much easier to be confident if you wear clothing that is formal and fits well. Dress confidently, and you are halfway home.

Appearance

The clothes you choose must fit well. Make sure you iron your shirt and pants, tuck in your shirt, button your buttons, fasten your belt, and tie your shoes. If you are missing something basic and it is noticed, you might lose a couple of points. However, if your suit jacket is three sizes too big or your pants are baggy, they might think that you will present a sloppy image to other people. Your appearance matters because the sales manager is trying to assess if you are going to fare well in front of prospects, customers, and their own management. I always recommend wearing the outfit you feel most confident in as best practice.

Shoes

Wear dress shoes or heels in an interview. If you wander down the hall to meet the CIO and she sees you in sneakers, she might make an offhand comment about your choice of shoes on her next call with the sales manager.

All you need is the CIO to jokingly ask Sara, "Is he the one who wore tennis shoes to the interview?" If this happens, Sara might subconsciously make the decision that you are not the best candidate. If you had worn dress shoes, maybe the CIO stays quiet. Dressing formally shows you are taking the company's job offer seriously.

There's a famous quote in The Shawshank Redemption where Morgan Freeman asks the question, "I mean, how often is it that you really look at a man's shoes? He's technically right. No one ever really looks at your shoes. Except in a sales interview, everyone looks at your shoes. To answer Mr. Freeman's question, "Not often, unless it's a sales interview."

Arrival

After you have packed your bag, dressed appropriately, and arrived on-site early enough, you will want to spend the rest of your time wisely before the actual interview. Most interviews are in an office, so let's use this assumption.

When you enter the lobby of the building, focus on greeting the receptionist and any other employees you encounter with a big smile. It is essential to greet everyone with a smile and a great deal of respect. It is important because you never know who that person may turn out to be.

A few years ago, I was headed to another city for sales training. I arrived early and picked out my seat in the conference room and then began wandering the halls trying to find the men's room.

When I was about to leave the restroom, a woman slammed open the door and hit me in the head. She had her head down and was rushing. She had no awareness of her surroundings and thought that she was entering the women's restroom. I stepped back and smiled despite the discomfort. We exchanged a laugh, and she instantly apologized. It really hurt, but I maintained my composure and played it off well.

Had this happened in downtown Manhattan, I might have had some choice words for her. But in a professional environment, I remained respectful.

We went on to chat for a few minutes about the ride in, traffic, etc. She apologized again, and we parted ways.

Halfway through that day's training session, our guest speaker was introduced. She was an Executive at one of our top customers, and she was also the woman who almost knocked me over in the men's room. When she came onstage, she included me in her opening remarks as she mentioned how nice the people were at our company.

It's imperative that you treat everyone you encounter with respect, and this is especially true on the day of your big interview.

Have the mindset that your interview could start as soon as you leave your house. Sometimes a security guard might be watching you, or that person behind you in line at Starbucks might work for the company. When you are in the vicinity of the office... you must be on your game. Take the same courteous, professional approach with each person you encounter when you are heading to your interview.

This will go further than any of those 30-60-90-day plans that everyone brings to an interview. Focus on the people you encounter, especially when you are arriving and leaving. These people are just as important as the person interviewing you. People talk to people, and people want to work with people they like. Sales is a people business.

Once you greet the receptionist, it is best to mention that you have arrived a bit early for your interview. Politely ask if they can hold off notifying Sara just yet. Tell them you are happy to wait in the lobby and then politely ask if there is a restroom you can use. Engage in small talk only if they are open to it, and remember to thank them once they point you in the proper direction.

John P. Davis

Manners with the front desk (and in general) are such an important part of my process. They are valuable in any interview process, but especially so when you're in sales. Most sales reps believe that their personality, charm, or relationship skills make them a strong rep. It's actually neither. **The most successful sales reps naturally have the best manners.** They do not fake them either. Be genuine with the front desk.

Why would you ask to use the restroom? Aside from the obvious reason, it is a great way to double-check things. You have just traveled in some capacity. Whether you have walked, driven, taken the subway, flew, hiked, or Uber-ed to this location, it took you a bit of time and effort to get here. You owe it to yourself to check your appearance in the mirror before your interview. This is a must.

If there is no restroom, you can check yourself out on your phone or perhaps in a mirror in the lobby. It isn't a fashion show but take a minute to ensure that you have not messed up your hair, your tie, or have something caught in your teeth. If you have your fly down for the duration of your interview, it may be more detrimental than embarrassing. I have a long beard, so I check it once or twice beforehand to make sure I do not have something stuck in it.

Try not to get caught checking yourself out on your phone's camera. If you do, try to play it off as if you are just checking yourself as a precaution. You do not want to appear narcissistic to the receptionist or others in the lobby while checking yourself out. A lot of sales managers will ask their colleagues about a candidate's behavior in the lobby. When you are on-site at the company you are applying to, you always need to use your best manners and be on your game.

What do you do in the waiting area at the dentist's office or the airport? You check your phone. What do you do in the waiting area for a sales interview? You <u>do not</u> check your phone.

This is very difficult for candidates. It will be extremely hard for you not to check your phone. You might disagree, but it is an important part of my process. If you are on your phone, you will not be on your A-game. Sara Jones could walk out early from around the corner, and her first impression of you will be that you are doing something unimportant on your phone.

Honestly, that would be an accurate impression on her part. There is a higher chance of you being on Instagram while you wait in the lobby versus doing actual work. Even if you are doing something productive on your phone, Sara Jones will assume that you are doing something insignificant.

When I see a candidate is on their phone in the lobby, it tells me that they're more interested in killing time than they are with people they may encounter. This is not how you would act in a prospect's lobby, and I have seen it firsthand work against a rep.

I was once in the lobby with one of my reps, and he was playing games on his phone. The CFO of the company walked by, and we exchanged a brief hello. The rep did not look up. When we went in for the formal sales meeting with the CFO, who do you think had a better first impression? Me or the rep? A smile and a hello can go a long way in a prospect's lobby. It can go even further in the interviewer's lobby.

You need to be professional while you wait. Be focused and present. Do not scroll through memes or check out the latest video from that trainer from your gym. Keep your phone in your pocket, and your chances of making a good impression with others around you will increase. Any interaction with someone in the lobby will be more beneficial than anything you could be doing on your phone.

More importantly, you might miss Sara's arrival and be caught entirely off guard. Stick to my process as best practice, and you will be ready to go at a moment's notice. Here she comes...

Greeting

Sara Jones is walking your way. You think it is her simply by the way she is looking at you. It is time to make your move. **<u>Stand up and smile</u>.** This not an option. You must do this. Many candidates do not smile when they first greet me. It is a deal-breaker. If you don't smile, you instantly appear cold, distant, and stand-offish.

If you are not comfortable with smiling when you first meet someone, it is critical that you practice smiling alone in a mirror. This will go a long way, not only in interviews but also for sales in general. A smile is how you should greet anyone in sales when you are meeting them for the first time. By smiling when Sara is approaching you, she will make the subconscious connection that this is how you will present yourself to prospects, customers, and her management in the future. This is a great subconscious connection for her to make. Remember that one of the four key items is having Sara vouch for you to her management. A smile increases your chances of that happening.

Extend your hand out and introduce yourself. Make sure to say her name. For instance, if she says, "Hi, I am Sara." You should say, "Hi Sara, I'm John Davis, nice to meet you." Or if she asks, "Are you John Davis?" You should say, "Yes, I am. It's nice to meet you, Sara."

My mom always insisted that I use everyone's first name. I hated it at first, but now I do it all the time. People love hearing their own name. Sales is a people business. You should be able to make the connection that Sara would love to hear you say her name. This is a must on your introduction to every salesperson you meet from here on out. It should be a must with every person you meet, but especially in sales.

This initial interaction is difficult to master because there are going to be a lot of unknowns and different iterations that play out. It is best practice to try to incorporate four basic items into your first interaction with Sara.

- Greet the person using their name. "Hi, Sara."

- Introduce yourself. "I'm John Davis."

- Acknowledge the encounter. "It's nice to meet you."

- Stand up and smile.

If you arrive on time, greet the receptionist, ensure you have dressed appropriately, and then you greet Sara using her name while standing up and smiling, you are ahead of 99.95% of the candidates who I have ever interviewed. You could already have the job, and I'm not joking.

These initial steps are fundamental, and still, somehow, they are often overlooked. In a sales interview, candidates are sometimes too focused on talking about their quota or how they closed a particular deal. Their mind is elsewhere when they meet Sara, so they discount the small things that truly matter.

Your vibe, your mood, your presence, and especially your first interaction with Sara will be remembered long after you leave that office. Don't discount the little things. They matter. Most salespeople will remember the interactions they had with you much more than your numbers.

The Walk

Once you greet Sara appropriately, you will begin the walk to the area where the official interview will begin. The walk might take only a few seconds, or it could be much longer down a series of hallways, past cubicles to the back-corner conference room. Regardless of how long the walk is, you must be social and personable without being dramatic or drawing upon any negativity. What do I mean by that?

If Sara says something about the building being built in 1940, you can ask if she likes it. Don't be bland. Don't just say, "Oh, yeah." Be responsive. It shows that you care. Be interested in what she has to say and even a bit inquisitive. But you do not want to say something like, "Oh, 1940. Right before World War I?" By saying something like this, even if you think it is innocent, you've indirectly started talking about World War I. Don't go down a conversational rabbit hole.

Even if nothing else is said about the war, Sara may think to herself, "Is this person a history buff?" You put it out there within the first few minutes of meeting her, and now it is out there forever. My brother put it best: you just have to be cool. Try to stay cool and low-key during the walk. There will be a lot of emotions and judgments going on. Respond to Sara and be personable, but do not say anything that could be perceived as dramatic or negative.

It is perfectly fine to accept an offering of water or coffee or even to hang up your jacket. It is perfectly fine to accept a mint or a million other little things that might come up, but you must be self-aware that you are not making too much of a scene. For instance, I offered a candidate coffee one time. He accepted my offer, and I was happy because I wanted one too. We went to the kitchen, and he kept fiddling over the different sugars, looking for a particular kind. We struggled to find the right one, and he was pretty bent out of shape.

It was a bad look for him because I only had sixty minutes to interview him and what I mostly remembered was his sugar antics. My thought process (and every good sales managers' thought process) is as follows: if my main recollection of this rep is the scene he made in the kitchen, I cannot imagine what memories he would leave imprinted on our prospects while on-site with them.

We, as sales managers, are judging you as if we were a prospect. The correlation between a sales process and a sales job application is very real. It is as real as it gets once you are in person. If I see him as "the fumbling sugar-man," our prospects will see the same, and perhaps they won't wish to spend money with him.

Another candidate refused to hang up her wet jacket and wanted to carry it with her. She went on to tell me that her jacket cost $2900, and she didn't want to be too far away from it in the office for so long. This was just odd to mention. It made me think that she had some deeper trust issues going on. After all, I didn't think anyone would steal her jacket.

This is what people do, though. We are all human, and we all make bad first impressions at times, just by our nature. Focus on not making a scene while trying to be social and personable while you walk. If you fail at this, Sara may label you as "Coffee Guy" or "Jacket Girl," and your chances of joining her team will start to diminish.

You need to remain true to yourself. That is why people tell you, "just be yourself." This is true, but if you have a tendency to make a scene before you sit down to talk, it is something you will need to work on. Actions speak louder than words. Be your best, relaxed version of yourself, and act appropriately on the walk to the interview room.

The Interview Room

You are now in the room--time for the interrogation. This is the mindset people usually have when they finally get into the interview room. This feeling is mainly due to nerves.

There is no need to be nervous, but I realize that nerves are a real issue so let me encourage you instead. Sara has invited you to talk. You just worked so hard over the past few days, weeks, and months to set up this meeting. You have earned this. Enjoy it. **This is your meeting.** You worked very hard to set it up, and Sara agreed. She is interested. People do not take meetings about things they are not interested in, and sales managers do not set up interviews with candidates that they are not interested in.

Candidates also associate interviews with interrogations because of their prior understanding of interviews. Most of their interviews have been interrogations. The interviews you see on TV or in movies are typically interrogation-style interviews. Your parents and friends fill your head with the difficult interviews that they have experienced.

Why is this the norm? Most interviews are conducted in a way that allows the interviewer to factually qualify and assess your credentials. In an in-person accountant interview, the interviewer might ask about your 3.1 GPA. They will want to know more about the rigorous accounting course work at your school and what you scored on the CPA Exam. The interviewer might also ask you to discuss different accounting principles and how they compare. They might ask about your thoughts on work-life balance so they can understand your willingness to work long hours during the busy season. They are trying to figure out if you would be a good accountant by asking about your qualifications.

The same is true in almost every industry. The interviewer wants to understand and push you on your credentials to see if you can back them up. It is impossible to effectively measure, compare, and verify credentials in a sales interview. Even if they dig into the 88% of quota attainment that you had at IBM, they are not going to be able to effectively compare it to someone who achieved 92% SalesForce. Do not let anyone try to tell you otherwise. **A sales interview should never be looked at as an interrogation. Instead, it should be looked at as a sales meeting.**

You didn't walk into an interview room. You just walked into a sales meeting room. You are now about to take part in a meeting that will decide if the company provides you with a job offer. How do you conduct this sales meeting effectively?

Mentally prepare yourself and understand that this is <u>your meeting</u>. You asked for it over and over through your prospecting efforts. You convinced Sara on the phone that this meeting would be valuable for her and persuaded her to agree. This is your meeting. <u>You run it</u>. You call the shots.

Most candidates make the mistake of assuming that this is Sara's meeting. This is wrong. A sales interview is the candidate's meeting, not the manager's meeting. Sara did not hunt you down and call you to set it up. You pursued her. You run the meeting.

Imagine if you secured a meeting with the VP of Finance at Walmart after trying for a month to get on her calendar. Now, imagine yourself walking into her office, sitting down in the chair, and just talking about the weather. Or better yet, imagine if you just sat down and looked at her without saying anything. Walmart's VP of Finance would think that accepting your meeting was a complete waste of time.

Why should it be any different with Sara? This is your exact moment to demonstrate that you know how to conduct an effective sales meeting. Conducting an effective sales meeting may be the most important part of the sales process. It is critical to demonstrate to Sara that you can run one. You can accomplish this very easily with a few key steps, but before we review them, you must understand the gravity of the situation.

You have just walked in for a sales interview. You are about to be judged on whether you can conduct a sales meeting. You will not be judged as much on your credentials as you will be on how you conduct this meeting. You must take control of the meeting right away, and you must do it before Sara does.

This is also the safest way for you to proceed. If you simply sit down and let Sara kick off the meeting, you will not have control of the flow. If you sit down and take control, you will be able to outline a flow that is favorable to you and get Sara to buy-in. This initial ownership of control is sometimes referred to as an upfront agenda. It is a basic sales concept that I will explain how to use it to your advantage when you walk in the room.

Upfront Agenda

Have you ever had the age-old dinner debate with your significant other--"What do you want to do for dinner tonight?" Once that question is thrown out there, a debate starts, and who knows how it will end. You offer up Mexican, and they decline. They ask if you want Italian, but you are not feeling it tonight. Suddenly, you are twenty minutes into the discussion when you really just wanted a pizza. Your significant other eventually agrees on pizza after an unnecessary argument that took forever. It happens all the time.

If you had provided an upfront agenda, you could have avoided the entire debate. An upfront agenda in that situation would look something like this: you finish work and call your significant other. When they answer, you say, "I'm pretty hungry and was thinking about dinner tonight. I'm going to go ahead and order a pizza to keep it easy. What do you think about that?" They agree, and you are golden. Your significant other may not always agree, but the point is you took charge and set out your agenda in a way that framed up your desired outcome, a pizza.

You provided your position and gave your significant other a chance to critique it by offering a modification. However, most people who are provided with an agenda upfront will follow your lead. An agenda is much more effective in a professional sales setting than it is with someone you are romantically involved with because there's less history between you.

Once you are in the interview room with Sara, you have the opportunity to take charge and set up your agenda. If you do not do this, Sara will typically throw out a topic that she is interested in, or she might say, "So, tell me about yourself." Some candidates think that is a good thing, and then they continue to talk about themselves for way too long. No matter what you think and no matter what Sara says or asks of you, she is looking for you to set an upfront agenda.

It does not have to be painfully long or formal, but you need to structure the meeting. Start with something simple. Even if Sara beats you to the punch, it is perfectly acceptable to still kick things off with an agenda.

"Absolutely, thanks for having me in today. I was thinking that we could start by letting me refresh you a bit about where I am in the process and how I got here today. Then we can open it up to talk more about the role. Is that okay with you?"

Sara will be blown away. Odds are, she has just interviewed three candidates earlier this week who immediately started talking about the weather once the door closed. Now here you are, demonstrating that you know how to conduct an effective sales meeting.

It seems so simple, but I am telling you that this will show her you know how to conduct a meeting. That's essentially all you need to accomplish. In the description of any sales rep, job duties include "must be able to conduct effective sales meetings." Your actions at the beginning of this meeting will carry you far beyond you can imagine.

I have interviewed candidates who sit down in the chair and kick off the meeting by telling me that they are already at 250% of their annual number. This is the equivalent of a car salesman approaching me at a dealership and saying, "I'm already over my annual quota." It is complete and utter nonsense. Would you ever tell a prospect that you are over your number? No. Why would you kick off a sales interview this way?

If a candidate comes in and has the sensibility and confidence to set up an agenda for me, I am always impressed. I am confident that if I hire them, they can go do the same thing when they meet with our prospects.

After the Agenda

Sara is more than likely going to buy into your agenda and let you start the conversation. If you have followed my process accordingly, you should be on cruise control at this point in the interview. Tell Sara a bit about what has happened so far and tie it into your story.

You have practiced your story many times and perhaps even told it to Sara already. If not Sara, you might have told it to another one of her colleagues in the initial stages of my process. There is no need to go on some long preamble about how motivated you are or how hard of a worker you are. You just want to refresh Sara about your story.

Think about it like this: you are a sales rep, and you just had a few phone calls and exchanged a few emails with a prospect named Sara. The prospect has invited you into her office, and you are now sitting together. It is only natural that you would provide her with a brief recap of the situation. You are recapping your story as a rep.

"So far, I have had a couple of conversations with people at Yahoo and provided them with my resume. You and I spoke briefly on the phone a couple of weeks ago about why I am looking to change roles (or to get into sales). It is part of my overall plan. As I mentioned, I started off…. *(insert a short version of your story)*. That's what got me here today, sitting with you. I am excited to be here and can't wait to hear more about the role."

Stop Talking

This should take you all of one minute. Maybe two minutes if there is a bit of interaction with Sara, but absolutely no more than two minutes. If you can't tell your story in one to two minutes at this point, you need to practice it again.

Everything up to this point in the interview can be somewhat rehearsed at your house prior to the interview. It should come out naturally and with some energy behind it. You do not want your story to come out monotone, and you never want to sound like a robot. Deliver your one-minute story with excitement (not too much) and show that you are truly happy to be here.

After the upfront agenda, quick recap, and your story, you should be about ten to twelve minutes into the interview. This is typically how long it will take when you include things like pauses, the walk, the greeting, etc. You only have about forty minutes left in this interview, and so far, you are proving that you can host a meeting and provide clear details as to what you are looking to discuss.

A Healthy Conversation and Redirection

Now it is time to just have a healthy conversation. Sara will thank you for the info (your story), and then she will start talking. At this point in the interview, we do not know what to expect from her. Every sales manager is different. The good thing is that most sales managers make an initial decision on whether to hire you within the first few minutes of meeting you. If you are able to stick to my process and make it to this point, there are good odds that you are in a strong position with Sara.

Sara and other sales managers all have their own style of interviewing. It is hard to prepare for every single type of interview, but these are some typical styles to be aware of. Some managers may conduct a behavioral interview where they ask you difficult and stressful questions to judge how you behaved in different scenarios. Others will conduct a conversational- or narrative-type interview where they ask you to talk about different scenarios and experiences that you have had.

Other managers will conduct what I call a "doctor's office interview." This is usually an interview filled with a lot of questioning. The questions are very direct, similar to when a doctor repeatedly asks, "Do you smoke? Do you drink? How much sugar do you eat?" In this style of interview, the sales manager is interested in gathering data for their analysis.

Some other managers may work off a script and try to be progressive with their interview style. They will ask you questions like "what type of animal would you like to be?" or "How many mice can you fit in a swimming pool?" This type of questioning is challenging your comprehension to see how you use logic to think and respond. Some managers will drill you on the specific product that you will be selling, or they will put you to the test and ask about your knowledge of the industry. This can be challenging for any candidate regardless of how much they prepare. There are still more interview styles out there that sales managers will use to supplement their analysis of you as a sales candidate.

Candidates frequently ask me to help them prepare with mock interviews. Some experts even host webinars and classes to help you through mock sales interviews. This is a waste of time. It is not possible to successfully prepare for every type of interview. Rather than prepare you for each style, I will provide you with a game plan that you can continuously come back to throughout the interview.

When I interviewed at Oracle, the sales manager asked me to describe every product that Oracle sold. I paused for a second and thought. Oracle has thousands of products. This was going to be very difficult to answer. If I started to describe any one of their products, the manager would ask me even more questions. Instead, I answered truthfully, "You guys sell everything that might take me a while." She laughed, and I did, too. We moved on to discuss the open role.

A sales interview is a game intended to test how you handle yourself in a meeting with a prospect. If you find yourself doing things like describing the difference between "being authentic" and "being genuine" or trying to solve some type of riddle about how many nickels you can fit in a garbage disposal, you are losing the game. In this instance, the sales manager is the prospect. They are trying to throw you off. They are trying to catch you in a trap and call BS. Why? It is their way of weeding you out. Be brave and tell them the truth.

For instance, if a prospect asked me, "Do you know every product we sell?" I would respond with, "I don't think I know them all. I can probably only cover the main ones, but I think we have an opportunity to help your company." During a sales meeting, sales reps have no problem with redirecting a prospect. So why do they have a problem redirecting sales managers?

Many candidates believe the sales manager is in a position of power, so they tend to subconsciously think that the sales manager is always right during the interview. This is a bad way to think. You have power in the interview, and you need to be honest and redirect the conversation when necessary. Redirect the conversation consistently (and professionally) towards discussing the open sales job. Remember, this is your meeting. It is not rude to effectively redirect a sales manager the same way you would redirect a prospect.

There are several questions that you should be asking Sara during your meeting. You want to know the territory, the commission rate, the previous attainment in the territory, and the length of a sales cycle. What is the target number of weekly meetings? Ask her what the average deal size is and what your annual quota would be.

These are all questions that you would want to get answered in a sales interview. Every great sales rep in the world would agree with me on that. If this is true, then why do we find ourselves describing which type of animal we are to the sales manager? We do this because we get nervous and we start playing their game. That question is pointless in a sales interview, and it is intended to be! The sales manager is trying to see if you can redirect a sales meeting.

When you meet with prospects, they are going to tell you all kinds of crazy things. They will talk about their kids, their car, the news, and a million other topics. They will ask you random questions about your industry and products or maybe even the stock market. The prospects do this because they are normal people and just like to talk. You are the sales rep. You are the one trying to sell them something. It is your job to refocus and redirect the conversation towards the desired outcome of the meeting: moving towards the next step. The desired outcome of a sales interview is also moving towards the next step: discussing a job offer. If you spend your time focused on answering every question thrown at you, you will run out of time and lose your chance at moving the ball forward with Sara.

There is no need to cut her off or be rude. There is never a situation where you have to act like a jerk to accomplish a redirect. This is true both in an interview and in a meeting with a prospect. If you are rude when you redirect a conversation, you are not going to sell much, and you are not going to get many job offers. Use your charm, wit, and personality to redirect and refocus.

Candidates that I've coached use redirecting all the time. They will call me after an interview and say things like, "He kept asking me to define my ideal vacation, and I redirected him. I said I'd tell him after we talked more about the open role… and he loved it!"

If you are new to sales or if you have not interviewed in a while, you might not realize that you should be taking charge of a sales interview. If you sit back and just answer question after question, you are not going to achieve much. You can certainly answer some questions, but it is important to redirect most of the conversation towards the task at hand.

Let's get back to the example with Sara in the room. The agenda is done, and the natural conversation of the interview has begun. You can answer some questions and have a bit of back and forth with Sara. When you feel the questions are becoming a bit scattered or off-topic, that's your cue to redirect.

- "What was your quota last year?"

- "I finished at 87% last year. What is the quota in this role?"

- "What type of car are you?"

- "I don't have a car right now, but I'd say that I'm a Toyota Camry at best. What about you? And does Yahoo sell cars?"

Those are a couple of examples that show how you can answer a question and still adjust a conversation at the same time. Redirecting is a natural tendency in any conversation. This is just another conversation, and the overarching goal is to redirect any off-topic questioning enough so that you have time to tell Sara you understand a sales process. A great sales rep can carry, shift, adjust, and redirect a conversation. You should do the same.

It sounds easy, but it can be difficult, depending on what Sara throws at you. If you are prepared to have this type of healthy back and forth and have this redirection framework in your back pocket, you will do just fine. If you are able to convey that you can run a sales process effectively and at the same time smart enough to learn the process at Yahoo, you are halfway home.

If you ever feel yourself going down a rabbit hole or talking too much about something that seems questionable, take a deep breath, and redirect the meeting. It is your meeting, and it is okay to do that. If you are unsure how to continue redirecting, it might be a good idea to ask some questions instead. I listed some earlier, but perhaps you just have a couple of questions off the top of your head for Sara. This is a perfect time and place to ask them. You do not always have to wait until the end of an interview to ask a question.

Once you are done with this conversational part of the interview, you might only have fifteen- to twenty-minutes left. That is a good amount of time. If you suddenly noticed that you only have two minutes left, you've had way too much conversation. Remember to always be cognizant of her time. It will go a long way in her evaluation.

Tell a Memorable Story

You need to tell a memorable story during your interview. It is a must. Remember when I said the sales manager needs to remember you? A memorable story will make that happen.

The best stories are 400 words or less. This means that your memorable story should be told in less than a minute and a half. If you are talking normally, at about three- to five- words per second, this will put you close to 400 words. You are not trying to tell Sara the plot of *The Green Mile*. You have limited time, and you need to ensure you share something memorable. If your story is too long, it will indeed be memorable. Sara will remember you as the person who wouldn't shut up.

Your memorable story is not <u>your</u> story. It is a story about why you are the best candidate for the job. It is your job to fit this into the interview. It does not have to appear out of the blue. It could come up naturally when she is asking you certain questions. "Why do you think you are the best person for the job?"

Candidates still believe there is a correct answer to that question. The truth is that your answer doesn't really matter at all. When a sales manager is asking you this question, they are giving you the floor and saying through metaphor, "Talk to me. Tell me a story. Entertain me."

This question is a good indicator that you should tell your memorable story. If you are not asked this question, it is your responsibility to work in your memorable story before the time runs out, and you are onto the question and answer portion.

What kind of 400-word story should you tell? Be creative. Think about this the night before your interview and practice it out loud. This is your chance and your moment that you worked so hard for, so just let your story fly. Don't be shy. Be open, be honest, and tell Sara a story that relates to why you think you deserve the job.

Relate this story to your sales-related activities, your ability to follow a process, or why you think you would be great working under Sara at Yahoo. You have to let your memorable story come out naturally. Talk about a time where you convinced someone to do something or that cool campaign you organized at your previous company. You could talk about a challenge you overcame or a story about trust or work ethic. Dig deep and find a **90-second** story about why you are the best choice for the job.

If you just start to explain that you are good at phone calls, you are toast. You need to tell a <u>memorable story</u> that describes the actions you took. People remember stories. They do not remember "I can…" and "I will…" Tell Sara a great, memorable story that she will remember later when she is considering who will be the best candidate for this role. If you can work in humor, mystery, or something captivating without going overboard, you'll make a positive impression. It doesn't always have to be so serious.

Sara may not remember your questions, comments, or even your quota achievements. Let's face it; she is a very busy person. Your story may be the only thing that Sara vividly remembers once you are done. Be sure to work it into the conversation when and where it feels appropriate. It should be, at the very least, a firsthand story that shows your character and eagerness to excel in this open sales job.

Questions and Answers

Let's say that you went a bit over on time so far and now have ten minutes left. Sara will most likely wrap up with, "That's about it. So, do you have any questions for me?" This is not an open invitation to ask 452 questions. You do not have time for more than one or two questions. What should you ask?

There is no reason to be shy here. I just caution you to use your intelligence as well. Don't ask about the salary. It is not an inappropriate question, but the timing is inappropriate. This would be like asking a prospect at the end of a meeting, "Do you have enough money to buy this?" Candidates who ask a sales manager about salary in an interview demonstrates that they are not self-aware or that they do not understand the hiring process.

Ask Sara questions about the sales position, so you have a better understanding of what working for her would be like. This is your future boss! It's Sara Jones! Ask her what she expects from you. Ask her how many reps on her team hit their number. Ask her what the best sales reps do better than the average sales reps. Ask her about the company or about senior management. Ask her what she thinks would be the best way to hit the ground running when you start. Things like salary, vacation time, working from home, expenses, and office culture are all types of questions that will be fielded later by someone in Human Resources.

Do some research on the company and learn Sara's perspective on it. Be excited and be curious. Don't ask, "What do reps wear in the office?" Things like that will put you in the "strange ranger" category. If the only thing that feels right is asking what the start date is for the job, then ask her that. Ask things that feel natural and be very cognizant of the time remaining. Think about what is appropriate to ask your future boss and then ask it with some excitement and energy. Sara will sense your enthusiasm, and it will go a long way.

Don't ask every single question I have listed above. They are just sample questions for you to review. It is fine if you do not have any questions if you had a genuine and thorough conversation. Ask one or two that you think you want to know and then end it. If you feel like Sara's answers are going to start taking you past the ten-minute mark, you might have asked the wrong question. It is on you to redirect and wrap it up.

In that instance, it is okay to interrupt and point out that time is almost up. A good way to do this is by saying, "Sorry to interrupt, but we only have a few minutes left, and I just wanted to be cognizant of your time." This is a polite way of doing it. She may insist she has extra time. If so, you can allow the interview to run longer. You must check, though, because you only asked for one hour and your hour is about to be up. After Sara finishes her final answer, it is on you to end the interview with an in-person close, just as you closed the phone interview.

Closing In-Person

Remember, closing is a simple and direct ask for something that you want. There is a high probability that you have already closed Sara or someone else on the initial phone interview. In that scenario, you were asking if it were okay to set up an in-person meeting. You do not need to ask for another meeting here. You just need to ask for her validation.

Just in case you are reluctant to close Sara, realize this: if you do not close her in person, you are going to leave the interview wondering what she is thinking. You will be left hoping to hear back from her on the next step. This is an awful feeling to have as a candidate. You do not know where you stand or what the process calls for next.

If a candidate does not try to close me in a sales interview, I do not even bother following up. I am not trying to be harsh. That decision is based on what the candidate has demonstrated to me. By not closing me, they have demonstrated through their actions that when they go on-site with a prospect, they are not going to close them, either.

This behavior is exponentially worse for me as the sales manager. Why? Now I will have a sales rep on my team who thinks it is okay to leave a sales meeting open-ended without a next step. This will result in me asking the rep repeatedly what the next step is in the sales cycle without an answer. The rep's sales process will continuously be stalled, and consequently, my business will stall as a result. Closing is an essential part of the sales process. Without it, you are just having a casual conversation. There is no selling involved because you are not being direct and asking for something that you want.

Keep in mind that if you do not close Sara, she will assume that you are incapable of closing a prospect and therefore, not fit to be a sales rep on her team. End of story. You must ask Sara for her validation and clarify the next steps. That's it. Once you do that, you are done interviewing.

So, how do you close? How do you ask for the job? There are a million ways to close Sara. You need to pick up on her social cues during the interview before you decide on how you will position your close. If you go in with an upbeat and peppy, "So, I am thinking we move forward with next steps Sara, you and I seem like a great team! Whaddya say?!" and Sara has not cracked a smile during the entire interview, it will not go well.

You want to accomplish two things with your close. You must confirm that she has no direct or obvious objections to you as a candidate, and you must confirm what the next step will be. The easiest and most efficient way to do this is to ask something like this: **"We're coming close to the hour now, and I want to be cognizant of our time. Is there anything that you see on your end that would prevent us from moving forward in the process?"**

This type of close is great because it addresses time management, asks about objections, and at the same time, acknowledges that this is indeed a process, and there are steps to follow. Some candidates try to close in person with a very hard close like, "Do you have any objection to hiring me on the spot?"

This hard close is not recommended because there are usually other internal steps that must get done, like speaking with her boss and with HR. Sara cannot decide right there and say, "I have no objections. Congratulations, you're hired." Also, the hard close is the equivalent of being on-site with a prospect and asking, "If you do not have any concerns, are you willing to buy my product right now?" It is a bit off-putting to close this way in an in-person interview.

Use a softer tone but make the ask. It shows that you recognize that there are more steps in the process and that you would like to start discussing them unless there is an objection.

Handling Objections

If Sara does not provide you with an objection to your close, you are free to discuss the next steps with her. Confirm the next step and ensure you understand what it is. It is not appropriate to push Sara or to make her commit to your desired next step. Your situation and your needs do not matter as much as the process Sara has to follow. She may have to speak with HR, her manager, other candidates, or close out the quarter before she can move forward with you. If she gives you a next step or a soft next step as we discussed before (i.e., talking to her admin), you just need to remember that step and thank her for her time. You are done.

If Sara provides you with an objection, this is your one chance to address it. Objections can come in many forms. Sara may say that she is unsure about your experience level, or that she is unsure of timing on her end, or that she's unsure about your past performance. These are all issues that you must address here in a proactive and healthy manner.

I emphasize "a healthy manner" because some reps handle objections poorly because of their ego. If Sara's objections hurt your ego, that is the sign of a bad sales rep. It could also stop you cold in your tracks as you look to move forward with her.

Imagine a sales rep is sitting with a prospect, and he asks them if they have any concerns before discussing the next steps. The prospect says, "You know what, I am just not sure if I love the Ford F-150." Or they say, "I just have to double-check the security package for your software because it doesn't seem up to par." These are two very common objections that could come up when a sales rep tries to close with a prospect. The biggest problem is not that the prospect has vocalized these concerns. The biggest problem is how the sales reps conduct themselves after the concerns are put out in the open.

What happens if the sales rep turns red and says, "What do you mean you do not like the F-150? I thought you loved it!" Or if the rep says, "Our security is top-notch! I already went through this with you, didn't you see that?"

The sale is dead.

The sales rep just let his or her ego get in the way. The prospect has now seen your true colors, and they are not going to feel very great. Once they see how defensive you have become, they might think something is suspicious about the deal. They might start thinking about if they even want to buy anything anymore. A lot of thoughts come up when someone is defensive in a sales environment.

If you react defensively to Sara's objections, guess what? She will make the connection that you are going to act like this with prospects. This is bad for business, and Sara just put another checkmark in her "concerns" column. Sara will see that you do not respond well to objections.

Understand that some sales managers will deliberately provide you with objections at the close just to see how you react. I sometimes do this with candidates, even if the interview is going very well. I might say something simple like, "It just doesn't seem like you are used to making phone calls." Then I pause and let them react to my objection. If they handle themselves appropriately, I will move on and assign the next steps. If they blow up and ask how I could think such a thing, I will keep pushing them to see if they blow up even more over a couple of other simple concerns.

It is all part of the hiring process in sales. The sales manager is trying to judge how you handle a sales process from start to finish. Even if they provide an objection or concern towards the end of your discussion, you must remain calm and address it professionally. Objections are part of every sales process. Their objection could be a test for you. If it is not a test, it could be a legitimate concern, but the objection itself is not as important as how you handle it.

Handle every objection professionally and politely and then put it aside. Never take it personally. I was in a sales interview, where at my close, the sales manager started walking towards the door and said politely, "I like you, John, but it seems like you are not a closer. Have a nice day."

I was about to get defensive, but instead, I stopped him and said, "Sorry. Wait for a second. I must not have done that correctly. I have been closing deals my entire life." He sat back down, smiling, and told me that it was just a test.

This is real life, and this is sales. The sales manager will most likely give you objections. Handle objections politely and professionally, then move on to address and confirm your next steps. You are well on your way to receiving a job offer.

Leaving the Interview

Now, there is little else you must do once you have closed Sara. After you are done, stand up, and smile. Thank Sara for having you in. Confirm the next step verbally with her and then walk out with her.

At this stage in the game, don't make a fool of yourself. Do not linger or try to revisit anything. Do not bring up anything else. Do not be that person who outstays their welcome or talks unnecessarily. It is just time to have some quick small talk as you leave. If you accidentally bring up something, she might ask you more questions. Stick to being cool and possibly talk about how nice the office looks.

Your time is done, and your goal has been achieved. If you happen to see any employee on your way out, thank them quickly and say goodbye with a smile. Leave with grace for the entire walkout. Keep it short and sweet and get out of there! Before leaving Sara, you must smile and shake her hand one last time. Forget this part and you can forget everything you've done up to this point. It won't matter; she won't hire you.

Thank-You Notes

What do you think your next step should be to make a great impression and stay top-of-mind? That's right. Send Sara a thank-you note. You must do this.

An email is absolutely fine. There is no need to send a handwritten note. The post office usually takes time, and it might be sent to the mailroom in a separate building that Sara never checks. There are too many variables with sending a handwritten note, so just send your thank-you note via email.

Reaching out to thank Sara can only help. It will improve, perhaps even solidify your chances of receiving a job offer. If you do not send a thank-you note, you will be going through many iterations of the sales job application process and wondering why the managers are not calling you back.

I am tired of interviewing seasoned sales reps who do not send thank-you notes. It is insulting. I just gave up an hour of my day to sit with you after you begged me to set up a time with you. I listened to your background and your story and had a good conversation about the opening on my team. Then you ghosted me. I can only assume that you are going to ghost our prospects after meeting with them. There is no way I will trust you with running a sales cycle in my organization.

One seasoned sales rep that I interviewed talked about how great he was at following a sales process, and although I loved hearing this, I wanted to see if it was true. At the end of the interview, I said, "It'd be great if you could follow up with an email that calls out your annual quota last year and where you finished. I know you are probably going to send a thank you, anyway. It doesn't have to be formal, but I'd like you to include that information in there." He was a seasoned rep, and he agreed. We both smiled and shook hands as he said, "No problem."

Two weeks later, he emailed me and asked where we were in the process. I responded politely and told him that I was moving on with another candidate. He emailed me back and wanted to understand what he had missed. I responded and told him that he never sent me the material that I had asked for, nor did he send a thank-you note. I also let him know that we both agreed to this follow up at the end of our meeting.

He responded immediately by apologizing and thanking me for my time and provided me with the material I had requested. He also included an excuse about how he had been so busy, and it slipped his mind.

Imagine if I had hired him, and he ghosted the CFO of American Express after a sales meeting where the CFO had asked for some follow up information. Imagine what the CFO of American Express would think of the rep. More importantly, what would he think of our company? I do not want that person to represent my sales organization.

Do you see the connection? The way you conduct yourself throughout my sales job application process says everything. Your credentials do not matter, but your actions and your process matter. Act professionally and send a thank-you note to Sara. Be sure to include any follow up that she may request. If you don't do this, you are just wasting everyone's time, including your own.

As we reviewed already, I encourage you to not only send a thank-you note to Sara Jones but also to <u>every single person involved</u> in the process thus far.

If you cannot figure out everyone's emails, try not to go out of your way to do anything extreme or unnatural to get in touch with them. But if you found a way of communicating with them via email, LinkedIn, or text, I strongly believe you will be able to do so again, and I suggest you send each person a thank-you note.

When you send the notes, you want to provide each person with a quick status update about what just happened, thank them for helping along the way, and let them know you are excited about the next step. Keep them short, positive, and authentic.

You will appear as a more polished rep by having these positive interactions with everyone you encounter.

This should be done during any future types of sales process you are involved in down the road. This is a very strategic method of follow up. When used appropriately, it will work wonders for you. If you just focus on a single relationship at a prospective company, your network will never be as wide as it could be, and your business may fail to scale. Focus on connecting with everyone you meet, and ultimately, your sales will be stronger.

The majority of sales job offers come directly via email in response to a candidate's thank-you note... Doesn't it seem like you should send one?

On my website, I provide additional information on best practices related to negotiating and accepting a sales job offer. I have found the situation to be very different for each candidate. Therefore it is difficult to address with a broad audience. If you have followed my process and now find yourself facing a job offer from Sara Jones at Yahoo (or from anyone else), congratulations! I encourage you to visit my site for help negotiating terms and conditions – but it's also okay to accept an offer on the spot.

If this is your first sales job, you have made a great career choice. If you were already working in sales in some capacity, I hope this is a big new opportunity for you. Wherever you are in your journey, I encourage you to revisit my process each time you find yourself searching for a new job. It will give you an edge over the competition and having *any* edge in sales is a huge advantage.

The Advantage

Sales is a very competitive field and because of this, reps look for any advantage that will put them ahead of others. Most reps start by examining their sales process. This is the most obvious place to look because it's the focal point of modern sales education. Whether it be podcasts, blogs, YouTube videos or books, there is a wealth of information available to reps on how to improve a sales process.

Any type of enhancement in this area will lead to more qualified opportunities, faster sales cycles and larger deals. In turn, sales process improvement is a major contributor to a rep's earning potential. This is a very well-known and agreed upon advantage in sales. You don't have to look too far to find material on how to improve your sales process. It is clear that this will lead to money in your pocket.

The second most common (but less obvious) area where reps look for an advantage is in the job itself. Every sales job seems to provide a more lucrative opportunity than the next. Factors like products, territories, quota, and compensation plans all have a major impact on a rep's earning potential. The problem is that it is nearly impossible to find a new product to sell while remaining in the same job. It is also very difficult to get a better territory or a better commission rate without changing jobs. Because of this, searching for a new job in sales is a regular occurrence among reps.

Most reps embark on a job search without a defined process in place. I have found that even the most process-oriented reps are a bit disorganized in their search. Looking for a new job can be intimidating, stressful, and make you feel like you're up against the clock. It's a big deal for most people and when it's time to search, it can be a lonely exercise. You most likely won't involve your colleagues or your management, because you'll want to get it done discretely. It is something reps do on their own. Unfortunately, there is very little material available to help reps with their search. Modern sales education just does not put any focus on it.

Improving your sales job application process is *just* as important as improving your sales process. Professional development in both areas will lead to more money in your wallet.

To date, I have not found much content, if any, focused on improving a sales job application process. While most sales education focuses on sales process improvement, my goal is to continue to offer guidance on the process of finding a new sales job. I find that having the *right* sales job can be just as rewarding as having the *right* sales process. I want to be a leading resource on this topic because I believe it to be an enormous earning opportunity for reps.

Becoming a sales rep has had a dramatic impact on me. It has given me the opportunity to directly influence my earnings and by doing so, improve the overall quality of my life. Although I have had such a positive experience, it did not happen overnight. I had to change companies, products, teams, managers and territories several times until I found the best fit. Throughout my journey, I stumbled, I learned, and I eventually succeeded in finding the right sales job for me. The same will be true for you.

In your sales career, you will find yourself searching for a sales job at different stages of life and for different reasons. While the circumstances may be endless, each time you find yourself searching for a new sales job, I encourage you to come back to my sales job application process. It will save you time and effort and it will yield lots of job offers. More job offers means more opportunities, more choices and inevitably, more money.

Pursue excellence in your sales job search in the same way you seek excellence in your role as a rep. You will learn this over time. For now, I think you are in the right place having just read my book and learned my process.

If you found any part of my process as valuable, I encourage you to share it with others in your network. Sharing information like this will reflect well on your brand as a sales professional. People around you who are in search of a sales job will be thankful and remember how much you helped them. Over time, your network of sales professionals will strengthen – another advantage.

I encourage you to visit my website at
www.howtogetasalesjob.com for more information.

I also encourage you to look for other areas where you can
improve your ability to earn more money. There is a lot of
information available and even the smallest advantage can help.
The first step for me was finding a job that paid commission.
Now that I have found it, I am constantly working hard to
improve other aspects of my professional life. I still believe my
dad was right, so I will leave you with the same advice - the
hard work will be good for you.

This book took me a while to publish. I am not a writer by heart
and I really appreciate your support. I wish I had known this
information when I was younger. Now that I do, I am sharing it
with you. Good luck in your search.

Best,

John

Works Cited

Dvorak, Doug. "How to Define A Sales Process for Sales Success," National Association of Sales Professionals, www.nasp.com/blog/how-to-define-a-sales-process-for-sales-success/. Accessed September 19, 2020.

Home Alone. Directed by Chris Columbus, performances by Macaulay Culkin, Joe Pesci, Daniel Stern, John Heard, and Catherine O'Hara. 20th Century Fox, 1990.

The Shining. Directed by Stanley Kubrick, performances by Jack Nicholson, Shelley Duvall, Scatman Crothers, and Danny Lloyd, Warner Brothers, 1980.

The Shawshank Redemption. Directed by Frank Darabont, performances by Tim Robbins, Morgan Freeman, Bob Gunton, William Sadler, Clancy Brown, Warner Brothers, 1994.

John P. Davis

Made in the USA
Columbia, SC
15 March 2022

57650828R00169